Montessori in Contemporary Culture

AMERICAN MONTESSORI SOCIETY
education that transforms lives

Montessori in Contemporary Culture

© 2024 American Montessori Society

Editors: Heather Gerker and Carey Jones

Published in the United States by the American Montessori Society (amshq.org)

ISBN: 979-8-35097-489-8

This book is dedicated to Dr. Nancy McCormick Rambusch, founder of the American Montessori Society (AMS); Dr. Peggy Loeffler; Dr. Gay Ward; and all past and present members of the AMS Research Committee, including current AMS research leaders Dr. Laura Saylor, Dr. Elizabeth Park, and Dr. Nanette (Sheri) Schonleber. We also honor all those who have supported the Montessori research movement throughout the years.

TABLE OF CONTENTS

PREFACE

In 1990, the American Montessori Society (AMS) sponsored a 3-day symposium entitled "Montessori in Contemporary American Culture." Two years later, topics discussed and highlighted during the symposium were organized and edited into a book (*Montessori in Contemporary American Culture*) by Margaret H. ("Peggy") Loeffler. The symposium (and the book):

> … examined the influence of Dr. Maria Montessori's ideas on the current American cultural and educational scene, more than eighty years after the initial introduction of her ideas in 1907 and thirty years after their second American entry in the late 1950s. (Loeffler, 1992)

This collaborative endeavor aimed to create a research agenda for studying the efficacy of Montessori education in the "new" century. With contributions from many distinguished scholars and experienced Montessori educators, including John Chattin-McNichols, David Elkind, David Kahn, Marlene Barron, Betsy Coe, and Sylvia Richardson, among many others, a vision was set, marking the start of many significant research-based initiatives.

Now, more than 100 years after the Montessori Method began, and almost 65 years after AMS's founding, it is time to revisit how Montessori education is shaping and being shaped by today's modern world. In 2023, AMS invited a group of esteemed scholars, experts, and practitioners to collaborate on a new project as it came together in two stages: 1) in a panel discussion at The Montessori Event 2024 in Orlando, FL, and 2) in the peer-reviewed chapters of this book.

AMS takes great pride in its role as a leading force in Montessori research. Since its inception, AMS has been a staunch advocate for and a significant funder of research initiatives to advance Montessori education. Our commitment to fostering high-quality research that enriches the existing knowledge about Montessori education is unwavering. The Montessori Research Facebook Interest Group is a platform for individuals interested in Montessori education to exchange research-related information, ideas, and opportunities. We also encourage individuals, regardless of affiliation or background, to contribute their Montessori-related research and scholarship to publications, including the *Journal of Montessori Research*, a free, peer-reviewed publication of AMS in collaboration with the University of Kansas.

As we celebrate the 65th anniversary of AMS in 2025, and mark over 30 years since the publication of *Montessori in Contemporary American Culture*, a book that has been a profound source of inspiration for this new project, we pay tribute to the vision of our founders and the dedication of those who paved the way for us. Their tireless efforts, commitment, and passion have played a pivotal role in shaping the Montessori Movement into what it is today. We hope this publication will inspire future generations, encouraging them to delve deeper into research and continue to advance Montessori education.

—The American Montessori Society, August 2024

INTRODUCTION

By Munir Shivji, AMS Executive Director

For six and a half decades, the American Montessori Society (AMS) has been at the forefront of Montessori education, dedicated to empowering educators and students through Montessori philosophy and practice. Our commitment to fostering a world where Montessori principles enrich the lives of children and their families has guided our work globally. This book, *Montessori in Contemporary Culture*, invites you to explore the evolution and impact of Montessori education, offering insights and guidance for today and the future.

In the 1950s, educator and parent Dr. Nancy McCormick Rambusch found herself dissatisfied with the traditional education system in the United States. Determined to find a better way for her children, she discovered the work of Dr. Maria Montessori. Her passion for Montessori education led her to reintroduce the methodology to the United States, culminating in founding AMS and being appointed representative of the Association Montessori Internationale (AMI) in 1960. By 1963, AMS had become the foremost Montessori association for professional educators, philosophers, physicians, parents, and the media. The rapid growth of Montessori schools across the United States, driven by a desire for educational reform, was a testament to Dr. Rambusch's vision, leadership, and potential.

Over the decades, AMS has evolved to address the changing needs of the Montessori community, establishing robust systems and commissions to uphold high standards for schools and teacher education programs. These initiatives include creating comprehensive accreditation and affiliation processes, developing professional development opportunities, establishing an international annual conference, and advocating for research to support Montessori pedagogy. Through the spirit of volunteerism and the dedicated work of those whose shoulders we stand, AMS remains a trusted pillar of support, communication, standard-bearer, and advancement for the Montessori Movement. We strive to ensure the Montessori pedagogy's relevance and impact in the modern educational landscape while protecting the integrity and essentials of the methodology. Today, AMS has grown to support over 22,000 members worldwide, including educators, teacher education programs, and schools, indirectly enriching the lives of countless children and families.

Drawing inspiration from Dr. Nancy Rambusch (1927–1994) and Dr. Margaret Howard ("Peggy") Loeffler (1921–2016), both luminaries in the field of Montessori education, AMS set out to explore how Montessori education is shaping and being shaped by today's modern world, using the 1992 version of *Montessori in Contemporary American Culture* as inspiration. We extend our deepest gratitude to all the contributors responsible for this new edition, *Montessori in Contemporary Culture* (2024). These individuals and authors are leading the way today in Montessori education worldwide in teacher preparation, school leadership, research, and leadership within AMS through service and advocacy. AMS is an entire ecosystem built over the years by the Montessori education community and continues to move forward in progressive and innovative ways thanks to the dedication and passion of individuals in this field, including those featured in this publication. Their efforts ensure that Montessori education remains vibrant and impactful.

The chapters in this book delve into various timely topics pertinent to 2024 and beyond, echoing themes of growth, innovation, and social responsibility. They cover the foundational principles of Montessori, AMS's historical evolution, and the importance of materials and the learning environment. The chapters also explore teacher training globally, the integration of Montessori in public schools, sustainability, social justice, parent engagement, public policy and advocacy, the balance between tradition and technology, and the future of Montessori education.

As you journey through this book, we hope you take away valuable insights and inspiration for your educational pursuits, empowering you to create meaningful and lasting impact in the communities you serve. We invite you to build upon this scholarship by engaging others in dialogue, advocating for Montessori education within broader educational and policy frameworks, and contributing your own research and insights. You will discover the collective conclusion from the authors of these chapters, which is that the essence of Montessori education lies in the social and psychological environment created for learners and their community rather than in the Method's more visible and unique artifacts. We encourage you to think critically and as you read, and to engage deeply (both personally and with your wider Montessori community) with the discussion questions that end each chapter. Montessori education has the potential to drive positive changes in our world, and you play an essential role in its continued growth and legitimacy. Embark on this journey with us, and let the power of Montessori education inspire you to make a difference. Together, we can cultivate a world where every child thrives in a nurturing and empowering educational environment.

CHAPTER 1

Upholding Our History:
Tracing Montessori from Past to Present

By Anna Perry, MEd

Dr. Maria Montessori (1870–1952), the Italian physician and educator who developed the Montessori Method, envisioned an educational system that would nurture the individuality and potential of each child. Her philosophy emphasized independence, freedom within limits, and observation as the primary tool to better understand and design supports for the child's natural development. Introduced in the early twentieth century, this novel approach contrasted with the received wisdom of traditional education and, when combined with Maria Montessori's public profile, became subject to widespread attention. Dr. Montessori and her Method quickly gained international acclaim, attracting educators from around the world who sought to implement her philosophy in their communities. Much has been written about the history and evolution of the Montessori Movement around the world. This chapter offers a brief history of its development in the United States, which led to the founding of the American Montessori Society, and emphasizes the importance of recognizing those who came before us. To do so, I introduce the idea that all of us working in Montessori today can (and should) trace our histories and connections within the Montessori Movement.

The Montessori Movement—From Italy to America

Born in Italy in 1870, Maria Montessori shattered societal norms by becoming one of that country's first female physicians. Her pioneering work with children with disabilities at the Orthophrenic School in Rome laid the groundwork for her revolutionary educational philosophy, and the founding of her first "Casa Dei Bambini" in 1907. In the United States, the adoption of Montessori principles came in the second decade of the twentieth century when notable enthusiasts such as Alexander Graham Bell, his wife, Mabel Bell, and Robert and S.S. McClure of *McClure's* magazine supporting initial efforts in private schools and wealthier communities (Loeffler, 1992). Early interest peaked in the 1910s and then waned due to a host of factors, including Maria Montessori's own disputes with some of her supporters, William Heard Kilpatrick's active disparagement of the Montessori "system" to the university-based academic community, and the advent of World War I. From the 1920s through the 1950s, interest in Montessori education ebbed, with few educators entering the field and fewer schools utilizing the Montessori approach.

The cultural sea change of the late 1950s and 60s marked a pivotal moment for Montessori education in the United States: it was a period termed "Montessori 2.0" (Debs, 2019, p. 52). America was experiencing significant social changes, most significantly the civil rights movement, the rise of counterculture, and increasing activism for environmental awareness and women's rights. These changes were rooted in a generalized view that traditional ideas required skepticism, interrogation, and improvement. Education was also to be interrogated, and, inspired by the growing interest in alternative educational models, a group of parents and educators, led by a young middle-class mother named Nancy McCormick Rambusch, came together to form the American Montessori Society (AMS) in 1960, effectively reestablishing the Montessori Movement in the United States. Phyllis Povell's 2010 book *Montessori Comes to America: The Leadership of Maria Montessori and Nancy McCormick Rambusch* adeptly provides a thorough and detailed history of the Montessori Movement's spread in the country, highlighting the assertive leadership of both Maria Montessori and Nancy McCormick Rambusch.

The earliest United States Montessori programs were privately run, but as the demand for alternative educational models grew, Montessori education also began to gain traction in publicly funded schools and programs. The first public Montessori programs opened in Milwaukee and Cincinnati in the early 1970s and were followed by others as many school districts struggled to address desegregation orders through the creation of magnet schools (Debs, 2019). The 1971 Supreme Court decision *Swann v. Charlotte-Mecklenberg Board of Education* created magnet school funding, which facilitated the founding of numerous publicly-funded schools designed to support racial integration experiences for students and families by providing unique educational opportunities for children, and managing their high demand with quotas that supported access for families of all different backgrounds. As these magnet schools were high-demand schools that operated without neighborhood school boundaries, families had to apply to be accepted. Many states started their first public Montessori schools in this fashion, including but not limited to Illinois, Texas, Connecticut, Louisiana, and Minnesota.

In 1993, Bluffview Montessori School in Winona, MN became the country's first Montessori charter school, and many publicly funded Montessori charter schools have since been authorized. Multiple Montessori programs have worked with Head Start, Early Head Start, and a wide variety of publicly funded Pre-K initiatives, which has allowed a much more diverse range of students to benefit from Montessori experiences. Today, approximately 10% of Montessori programs operate using public funding and/or primarily reach underserved communities.

As AMS's founder, Nancy McCormick Rambusch (1927–1994) played a crucial part in unifying and orienting Montessori parents, educators, schools, and supporters to a non-profit organization dedicated to promoting Montessori principles and practices. Her visionary leadership and advocacy efforts helped raise awareness about the benefits of Montessori education, leading to its widespread adoption and growth in schools across the country.

Rambusch's contributions also extended to curriculum development, nurturing the development of teacher preparation programs and research initiatives, and shaping the quality and standards of Montessori education in America. Her lasting impact continues to be felt in the thriving Montessori community and the ongoing evolution of Montessori education as a respected and influential educational approach.

Rambusch was a dynamic speaker, a passionate educator, and a strong advocate for more access to Montessori education for all children. She frequently acknowledged that the early success of AMS relied on the important contributions of other Montessorians. In the second wave of the Montessori movement in America, there were many people who had come into their own discovery of Montessori education: some through Rambusch and AMS, others via Maria Montessori and her various training courses in Europe and India, and still others trained by the people prepared in those original Montessori courses. Many of these new educators in this second resurgence of interest in American Montessori education were immigrants themselves, carrying the work forward to serve their new communities. As dedicated and tireless advocates for the Montessori Method, they influenced countless teachers and children and received local or even national recognition.

To Those Who Came Before Us

The "six degrees of separation" principle, which posits that any two people are connected by six or fewer social connections, can be intriguingly applied to Maria Montessori's lasting influence (Karinthy, 1929). The principle can show how the work of a few individuals had immense ripple effects on the lives of children, families, and educators. In the following paragraphs and in Figure 1, I outline a web of Montessori connections that dates from the mid-twentieth century to today.

Figure 1.

A Web of Montessori Connections

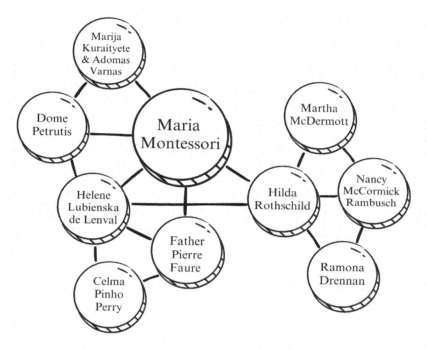

In the 1950s, while **Nancy McCormick Rambusch** was working toward her Montessori certification in London, **Marija Kuraityete Varnas** and her husband, professor **Adomas Varnas**, were launching an informal Montessori program in their Chicago home, together with their close friend and collaborator, **Dome Petrutis**. In 1958, they founded the Lithuanian Montessori Society of America. In the early 1930s, the three educators had participated in two Montessori training courses in Nice, France, led by Maria Montessori and assisted by **Father Pierre Faure** and **Helene Lubienska de Lenval.** The Varnases and Petrutis then opened several European schools before immigrating to the United States during World War II. After arriving in Chicago, they worked for several years in a factory, studying English on the side, while saving enough money to start a small Montessori program for other Lithuanian immigrant families. In 1963, they opened the Žiburėlis Lithuanian Montessori School, which continues to serve children in the Chicago suburbs to this day (Lithuanian Archives Project, 2015). Petrutis also worked with many Montessori teacher education programs around the country, including Midwest Montessori Teacher Training Center (MMTTC) and Seton Montessori Institute.

Hilda Rothschild, a strong advocate for early childhood education, ending poverty, and serving children with special needs, founded Xavier University's teacher education program in 1965 in her adopted hometown of Cincinnati, OH (Donahoe et al., 2019). A Jewish woman from Germany, Rothschild had graduated from the Sorbonne in Paris in 1934, and, in the early 1930s, also trained with Maria Montessori and Lubienska de Lenval there. She taught in Montessori schools in France, but left quickly in 1941 to avoid the Nazis and, once in the United States, worked in several school settings before launching the country's first master's degree in Montessori education at Xavier University, where she was a faculty member. Rothschild was a collaborator of Nancy McCormick Rambusch, particularly when it came to teacher preparation.

Martha McDermott, a native of Scotland, was trained by Muriel Dwyer and Claude Claremont in London in 1959, and immigrated to Cleveland, OH to teach, and was later hired by Xavier to teach at the Early Childhood level. (She would later take her Elementary training in Bergamo, and bring it back to the United States.) McDermott and **Ramona Drennan,** then director of the Montessori Education Program at Xavier University, teamed up with Rothschild and Rambusch to launch one of the nation's first public Montessori schools, Sands Montessori, in Cincinnati in 1975. Its success paved the way for several other public magnet schools to open between 1975–1994. This included the landmark 1994 launch of Clark Montessori, the nation's first public Montessori high school. Since that time, Cincinnati Public Schools have opened more Montessori programs: four more magnet schools, one neighborhood elementary school, and one additional high school.

My mother, **Celma Pinho Perry,** was born in Rio de Janeiro, Brazil, and left her home country at 18 to become a sister with Notre Dame de Sion outside of Paris. There, in the late 1950s, she trained as a Montessori teacher with

Lubienska de Lenval and, in the early 1960s, was prepared in the art of teaching teachers by Father Pierre Faure (Perry, C., 2015). With this dual training under her belt (unique at the time), and excited by the burgeoning Montessori movement in the United States, Perry immigrated to the United States in 1965. In New York, she met with Nancy McCormick Rambusch and Cleo Monson, Nancy's capable assistant (who would soon become AMS's first national director). Subsequently, Perry settled in Chicago, where she was hired by a passionate group of parents to design and found Seton Montessori School, a one-room schoolhouse for 3–6-year-olds on a rustic campus. With her background in teacher education, and realizing that the growth of Montessori education drove a need for qualified teachers, Perry founded MECA-Seton, now Seton Montessori Institute. She continued this work into the 2000s, joined and supported by her Montessori collaborator and husband Desmond Perry, himself an Irish immigrant.

The life and work of each of these remarkable Montessori influencers have had a lasting legacy, refining educational practices and shaping the lives of countless educators, families, and children in the United States and beyond who have benefited from the empowering and nurturing environment of Montessori classrooms. But there are many more "six degrees of separation" out there: every person involved in Montessori education today has been brought into this work and educated or influenced by at least one person who was in turn educated or influenced by a Montessorian who came before them—dating all the way back to Maria Montessori herself.

Through the work Maria Montessori began over 100 years ago, and the continued efforts of countless dedicated educators and advocates over the years, Montessori principles have permeated conventional education and even transcended education itself; aspects of Montessori show up in conversations about child development, adult learning theory, dementia care, and business. Montessori's ideas have been embraced in diverse communities and settings, from public schools to private institutions, further illustrating the interconnectedness of her legacy and the widespread adoption of her Method in the United States.

As we go forward in this book to discuss Montessori in contemporary culture and how the Method will continue to grow in the future, let us also remember the influence of those who came before us, and recall whose shoulders we stand on to serve the children and adults with whom we work. I invite you to trace your own Montessori journey back decades—perhaps even all the way to Maria Montessori herself. Who has supported and influenced you? How does your pathway back to the past shape your perspective on the Montessori approach today? How will the actions you take going forward influence those Montessorians who come after you? Through learning from the past and taking action for the future ahead of us, we will be able to build a better world through Montessori.

> As we go forward in this book to discuss Montessori in contemporary culture and how the Method will continue to grow in the future, let us also remember the influence of those who came before us, and recall whose shoulders we stand on to serve the children and adults with whom we work.

References

Debs, M. (2019). *Diverse families, desirable schools: Public Montessori in the era of school choice.* Harvard Education Press.

Donahoe, M., Kugler-Ackley, J., & Vertuca, M.L. (2019, October 4 issue). Montessori Public. https://www.montessoripublic.org/2019/10/public-montessori-gets-its-start-in-ohio/

Karinthy, F. (1929). Chain-links. Everything is different, 21–26.

Loeffler, M. H. (1992). *Montessori in contemporary American culture.* Heinemann.

Lithuanian Archives Project. (2015). Žiburėlis Lithuanian Montessori collection finding aid. https://owl.purdue.edu/owl/research_and_citation/apa_style/apa_formatting_and_style_guide/reference_list_electronic_sources.html

Montessori, M. (2012). *The 1946 London lectures.* Montessori-Pierson Publishing Company.

Perry, C. (2015). *Living, creating, sharing: A Montessori life.* Parent Child Press: A Division of Montessori Services.

Povell, P. (2010). *Montessori comes to America: The leadership of Maria Montessori and Nancy McCormick Rambusch.* University Press of America.

CHAPTER 2

Research and Observation: Pedagogical Essentials for Building a Better World

By Jana Morgan Herman, MEd, and Laura Saylor, PhD

Times have changed, and science has made great progress, and so has our work; but our principles have only been confirmed, and along with them our conviction that mankind can hope for a solution to its problems, among which the most urgent are those of peace and unity, only by turning its attention and energies to the discovery of the child and to the development of the great potentialities of the human personality in the course of its formation.

(Montessori, 1967, p. x)

Dr. Maria Montessori's legacy as an activist, scientist, and educator is a testament to her relentless pursuit of understanding human development and fostering learning environments that best support that development and, ultimately, peace in our world. Her journey began with overcoming societal barriers while studying medicine in the late 19th century. Undeterred by challenges, Montessori delved into research, particularly with children, laying the foundation for her groundbreaking work in education and peace, beginning at the Orthophrenic School in 1900 and later in 1907 when she opened her first Casa dei Bambini in Rome.

Montessori's approach emphasized the importance of scientific questioning, observation, and methods of education determined by those practices. In *The Absorbent Mind*, Montessori wrote,

There must be only one method of education. The method which helps the natural laws of growth and of development, alike for all. This is not an idea; it is a fact; an evident fact and it shows that it cannot be a philosopher or a thinker to dictate this or that method of education. The only one who can dictate the method is nature itself which has established certain laws, which has infused certain needs into the growing being. It is the aim of satisfying these needs, seconding these laws, which must dictate the method of education; not the more or less brilliant ideas of a philosopher. (1995b, p. 39)

Here, Montessori is telling us that science, and only science, must dictate methods of education. Indeed, this is how she developed her own Method. During the years that Montessori education proliferated in Italy, Europe, and beyond, many educational theorists and philosophers put forth new ideas about education, including the suggestion that all aspects of learning naturally develop on their own and that instruction from adults was unnecessary. This stands in contrast to Montessori's studies, which revealed the importance of direct (yet subtle) and intentional guidance from educators, such as the salient role of the educator in creating a prepared environment for the purpose of molding behavior and developing the intellect. Montessori's prepared environment is based on systematically observing children and understanding how they develop. Rather than adopting a hands-off approach, Montessori encouraged educators to actively and systematically observe and analyze the effects of the environment on children's behaviors and learning—this was quite different from some of the emerging educational philosophies and theories of the time.

Intellectual curiosity and systematic inquiry were not only integral to Montessori's ideas about education; they were central to her concept of pedagogy for peace, and they were characteristics she believed were essential for educators and students, "The child who has never learned to work by himself, to set goals for his own acts, or to be the master of his own force of will is recognizable in the adult who lets others guide his will and feels a constant need for approval of others" (Montessori, 1992). For Montessori, this is where world-changing work began. By ensuring that children learn to work independently, to be curious seekers of knowledge, and to have self-discipline and self-control, we will see adults who live lives according to what they have critically determined as right and just for the common good. Montessori's legacy challenges educators to embrace a scientific mindset, constantly evaluating new findings and knowledge, thereby fostering a culture of intellectual curiosity and growth essential for addressing complex societal challenges (Sackett, 2016). As educators, we can shape minds and instill values prioritizing empathy, understanding, and social justice. As educators and scientists, we can commit to constantly evaluating and challenging existing norms and systems, and asking ourselves tough questions about the impact of our curriculum, pedagogy, and classroom environment on fostering critical thought, understanding, and empathy.

Montessori's Scientific Pedagogy: Pioneering Education for Peace through Inquiry

Despite facing obstacles as a woman pursuing medicine in the late 19th century, Montessori persisted, earning her degree in 1896 and immersing herself in research with children, particularly those with disabilities. In 1900, she was appointed director of the Orthophrenic School, where she applied her scientific methods to develop educational approaches tailored to children's individual needs. This marked the beginning of her journey towards scientific pedagogy, a concept current in the study of education at this time. By meticulously collecting and analyzing data from her work, Montessori refined her educational practices, some of which would later be adapted to more conventional educational settings. From 1901–1906, Montessori delved into philosophy and anthropology, furthering her "scientific pedagogy" and her work that began in 1907 when she opened the Casa dei Bambini, overseeing the care and education of approximately 55 children of working parents in Rome's San Lorenzo district (Kramer, 1976). In her 1946 London Lectures, nearly 40 years after the opening of her first classroom, Montessori said,

Before we can give help, we must understand; we must follow the path from childhood to adulthood. If we can understand, we can help and this help must be the plan of our education: to help man to develop not his defects, but his greatness.

She continued,

Although this method bears my name, it is not the result of the efforts of a great thinker who has developed his own ideas. My method is founded on the child himself. Our study has its origins in the child. The method has been achieved by following the child and his psychology. (Montessori & Haines, 2012, pp. 6–7)

Montessori's scientific mindset permeated her approach to teaching. Ginni Sackett, in her presentation "The Scientist in the Classroom: The Montessori Teacher as Scientist" (2016), emphasized the importance of constant questioning and observation without rigid ideology, and urged Montessorians to adapt to new discoveries while remaining true to the Method's core principles. Sackett invited us to reflect on these questions:

Are we the custodians of an ideology that can only justify and dictate an educational practice that is frozen in another time and place? Or are we the caretakers of proven ideas that guide us to constantly question, to constantly observe, in order to recognize reliable evidence of both expected and unexpected phenomena as they occur in our scientific laboratories? (p. 16)

These words and questions have a place in each of our classrooms and workspaces. Our children and our world need us to question, study, engage in meaningful discourse, share effective research-based methods, and challenge one another's thinking. Independent thought, for Montessori, was a key element to creating a socially just world; as she explained in *Education and Peace*, true individuality is only achieved when one can act independently (Montessori, 1992). Montessori's legacy challenges educators to embrace a scientific mindset, constantly evaluating new findings and knowledge. We posit that Montessori's scientific approach in education was always intended to extend beyond the classroom—to foster a culture of inquiry and critical thinking essential for addressing complex societal challenges and the creation of a more peaceful world "The child is both a hope and a promise for mankind" (Montessori, 1992). As Montessori did throughout her life, we would be wise to maintain curious stances and independent thought that places a high value on science.

Fostering curiosity and independent thought is vital for promoting peace and understanding. This can be achieved through learning approaches that encourage students to ask questions, challenge assumptions, and explore perspectives. Critical literacy skills are essential for students to discern between fact and opinion, identify bias, and engage in respectful dialogue on controversial issues. Well-planned, collaborative projects can bring students from different backgrounds together to foster mutual understanding and appreciation for the diverse world we live in. By empowering students to become advocates for a more equitable and just world, we create opportunities for them to take action and create positive change in their communities and beyond.

Montessori Principles in the Evidence Base and Contemporary Culture

Montessori principles are increasingly applicable in today's dynamic educational landscape. As educators confront the lasting impacts of trauma on children and better recognize neurodiversity as a factor that affects learning, the need for informed observation and holistic support becomes increasingly apparent. Montessori's scientific approach to education, rooted in her extensive research and emphasis on the prepared environment, offers valuable insights into fostering nurturing classrooms that greatly aid children's development. Educators can create environments that nurture autonomy, independence, and social skills by aligning with trauma-informed approaches and prioritizing the integration of Practical Life activities, language development, and intellectual exercises. However, this necessitates a shift from academic rigidity towards a more balanced approach incorporating

By embracing Montessori's scientific pedagogy and considering it in light of current research findings, educators can cultivate transformative learning experiences that empower children to thrive and reach their full potential, laying the foundation for a more just and compassionate society.

outdoor play, hands-on experiences, and community engagement. By embracing Montessori's scientific pedagogy and considering it in light of current research findings, educators can cultivate transformative learning experiences that empower children to thrive and reach their full potential, laying the foundation for a more just and compassionate society.

Observation as a Cornerstone of Scientific Pedagogy

Instead of focusing on a set curriculum for the child at predetermined dates, the Montessori Method depends on individual readiness. Readiness is determined by the nuances of development in the activity the child engages in. This seemingly simple edict (When do you give the lesson? When they are ready?) is actually Sisyphean in nature and requires that first, adults doing the observing have engaged in a long, arduous path of unearthing and divesting themselves of their own experiences, beliefs, and biases about learning.

Teachers in training are often tasked with observing. Still, the ambiguity surrounding how and what to observe leads them to feel a need for more time, as they perceive observation as merely watching rather than engaging in the deeper, more nuanced sense that Montessori intended. In *Spontaneous Activity in Education* (1917b), Montessori says that adults often watch children just as they look at the stars. We can see they are beautiful and full of potential. But it is not enough to believe they are beautiful. We must learn to see the children as an astronomer sees the stars; each one is beautiful, yes, but astronomers have a deep knowledge of the stars, and which ones are, in fact, stars, and which are galaxies, nebulae, and clusters, novas, or planets. The vast array of objects we admire in the sky are far more interesting than our untrained eyes can behold. Our task is to know the intricacies of child development and overlay that knowledge onto the individual children in our orbit. Learning to observe this way requires an indefatigable effort of preparation, long before we begin observing children.

Though we often focus on materials and lessons for our observations, Dr. Montessori spent more time discussing the adult's attitude and how our adult interactions place barriers in the child's path toward normalization. She was fond of symbolism and used biological science to help us understand how every movement, even breathing or watching a child, may interfere with their natural development. She invited us to reframe our task to focus on the environment first and foremost to support a spiritual womb that nourishes and protects the child's development.

The prepared environment is not disconnected from our observation work, but is instead the singularly most important ingredient that allows us to identify and recognize the smallest incremental growth. This does not mean, however, that the activities are most important and that we should change our tray work every few weeks to inspire the children to engage in activities; quite the opposite! To create an environment suited to development, we must prepare a place without barriers, where every single thing and every nuanced movement by the adult must be consciously decided.

So, how are we to teach teachers to observe? Montessori wrote,

> The vision of the teacher should be at once precise like that of the scientist and spiritual like that of the saint. The preparation for science and the preparation for sanctity should form a new soul, for the attitude of the teacher should be at once positive, scientific and spiritual. (1995b, p. 107)

In her discussion of observation in education, Montessori emphasizes the distinction between seeing and true observation, highlighting that perception, rooted in knowledge, is crucial, as evidenced by the insights gained from observing children's movements and seeing how even minor adult interventions could profoundly affect a child's development.

In order to develop the ability to observe as scientists observe, we must first become aware of and control ourselves. Our impulses create or reinforce barriers to the child's growth. In our work with adult learners, we must spend more time developing the skill of observation beyond the goal of preparing the next lesson so teachers understand that their not observing correctly is the barrier to the polarization of attention and the path to normalization. Montessori believed that "normalization" is how children naturally behave if they did not have barriers placed in their way by adults. Today, a normalized child would look the same as one in Montessori's time, because children's brains and development have not changed. Technology is always changing, advancing, and pushing our realities into new understandings. The child's brain, however, needs the same things to flourish—namely, caring relationships with at least one adult, free play, and having their basic needs met. Normalized children who have those building blocks, and aided by a well-prepared environment,

> Show in their subsequent development those wonderful powers that we describe: spontaneous discipline, continuous and happy work, social sentiments of help and sympathy for others. Activity freely chosen becomes their regular way of living. [This] is the doorway to a new kind of life. (Montessori, 1995b, pp. 206–207)

It is also interesting to note that Montessori first instructed the teacher to systematically study themself "so that he can tear out his most deeply rooted defects, those in fact that which impede his relations to children" and discover his "subconscious failings" (1966, p. 149). "Put another way: "First remove the beam from your own eye and then you will see clearly how to remove the speck from the eye of the child" (1966, p.149). Only after Montessori admonished teachers to check themselves earnestly did she begin to describe the behaviors and tendencies we might see in children, deviations that will feel familiar to teachers in Montessori classrooms today: including "inconstancy, wavering attention, untidiness, disobedience, sloth, greed, egoism, quarrelsomeness, instability, and the flight from reality, fugues, where the mind, which should be building itself up through voluntary physical activities, then *takes refuge* in fantasies, becoming absorbed in images and symbols, and moves restlessly about" (1966, p.155). The ways Montessori described children are no different than what we see in children today. What *is* different are the adult interactions in children's lives. In our concern for children's safety, we micromanage almost every aspect of their existence; we fail to see how our own actions, not just technology or a global pandemic, impact children in significant ways.

The barriers we have placed in front of children today are grounded in the lack of play and over-intervention in the actions of adults, which prevent the free activity of the child, such as when Montessori described that the "conflict between child and adult begins when the child reaches a stage in his development when he can act independently" (Montessori, 1966, p. 72), and that adults begin to limit the child's freedom, even down to requiring the child to sleep even if he is not tired. "An adult who forces the child to sleep more than he needs is unconsciously forcing his own will upon the child through the power of suggestion" (Montessori, 1966, p. 73). Montessori directs that children should be permitted to sleep when tired, wake when rested, and rise when they wish. How many caregivers today do that? She advises:

> Adults must become convinced that they have a secondary role to play in a child's development. They must endeavor to understand children so that they can properly assist them. This should be the aim and desire of a child's mother as well as all those who have anything to do with his education. A child is naturally much weaker than an adult. If he is to develop his personality, it is necessary that the adult should hold himself in check and follow the lead given by the child. And he should regard it as a privilege that he is able to understand and follow him. (Montessori, 1966, p. 75)

Montessori advocated for a profound self-awareness in education, urging educators to confront their unconscious biases and emphasizing the necessity of observing oneself before attempting to observe others as part of a broader effort to dismantle ingrained prejudices that may influence interactions with students. This introspective journey entails documenting personal behaviors, restraining impulses, and acknowledging the pride or ego that can distort perceptions, all with the aim of fostering genuine observation and understanding of children's needs and development. As we attempt to wipe our biases from the lenses with which we observe children, we must also recognize our pride, the ego; perhaps it could even be considered part of a savior complex that also interferes with our observations of children (Montessori, 2016).

Often, teacher education programs cover observation with the goal of helping new teachers understand what work the child has mastered and is ready for. The next level of observation may be expanded to include what factors may be driving or influencing a specific behavior resulting from something or someone in the environment. Both are good to know, but unless we start with the teachers themselves, we will miss the mark and render any observation incomplete.

Observation and Today's Child

Current research shows that children who experienced or witnessed trauma before 2 months of age seem to show long-term impact from those experiences, even if they have healthy and functioning experiences from 3 months on (Lyons-Ruth et al., 2017). Teacher education programs must talk about recognizing a constellation of behaviors that may be related to post-traumatic stress disorder (PTSD), complex post-traumatic stress disorder (CPTSD), neuroatypicality/neurodivergence, learning differences, and autism, to name a few. If we merely look at a child's behavior and make plans for lessons or redirection, we fall short in our work as scientists. If we wish to be scientists, we must have a foundation on which to base our observations, and our observations must be informed by the best and most current research in early childhood development.

In recent years, our understanding of trauma seems to be catching up with Montessori's belief in the healing powers of order, relationship, freedom, consistency, and the power of play in helping children recover from trauma or the "mental lesions" resulting from experiencing a traumatic event. Montessori writes,

> The wounds, which I call the wounds of degeneration, are mysterious. They are wounds of the nervous system.... The younger the age of the child when this lesion comes, the greater the danger of his future life; when this shock comes or lesion comes during the prenatal period, it is even more dangerous.... So we must foresee in the effects of this war the dangers for the new generation. (Montessori, 1917, p. 39)

Whatever the child experiences forms his identity. Those who wish to be the most effective Montessori educators must have training on the effects and impact of trauma and further must learn how to prepare and maintain a classroom that is more conducive to healing and less focused on academic achievements. If our observation does not center around the individual child's broad experiences, they are incomplete. We prepare ourselves by knowing all we can about ourselves, knowing the child, and observing with a keen eye as the child moves in the environment: we see the way children respond to loud noises, the requests or demands other make on them, if their level of concentration is alignment with what we typically see in their peers, if they are picky or ravenous eaters or if they sneak food even though there is no need, how they respond to redirection, if they are slow to move or never stop moving, if they easily make friends or if they seem to annoy their peers, if they recognize when they have mucus or dirt on them or if they are oblivious, if they seek oral stimulation from chewing their sleeves, hair, or mouthing materials, if they are sensitive to sensorial feedback like being bothered by tags or if they walk around with one shoe off and one shoe on without noticing, if they take care to tuck in their clothes or if they do not notice soaking wet sleeves. These behaviors, which we've all seen, give us clues about what the child needs from us.

We also need to further our understanding of the significance of Montessori's schedule of the day which is aligned with research on early childhood experiences and is crucial for educators aiming to create environments conducive to healing trauma. Montessori's proposed winter schedule, as shown in Figure 1, emphasizes Practical Life exercises, intellectual activities, physical exercises, free and directed games, manual work, and collective activities, all integrated seamlessly to support holistic child development.

Figure 1

Montessori's Proposed Winter Schedule of Hours in the Children's House

Opening at 9:00am – Closing at 4:00pm	
9:00 – 10:00	Entrance. Greeting. Inspection as to personal cleanliness. Exercises of practical life; helping one another to take off and put on the aprons. Going over the room to see that everything is dusted and in order. Language: Conversation period: Children give an account of the events of the day before. Religious exercises.
10:00 – 11:00	Intellectual exercises. Objective lessons interrupted by short rest periods. Nomenclature, Sense exercises.
11:00 – 11:30	Simple gymnastics; Ordinary movements done gracefully, normal position of the body, walking, marching in line, salutations, movements for attention, placing of objects gracefully.
11:30 – 12:00	Luncheon: Short prayer.
12:00 – 1:00	Free games.
1:00 – 2:00	Directed games, if possible, in the open air. During this period the older children in turn go through with the exercises of practical life, cleaning the room, dusting, putting the material in order. General inspection for cleanliness: Conversation.
2:00 – 3:00	Manual work. Clay modeling, design, etc.
3:00 – 4:00	Collective gymnastics and songs, if possible in the open air. Exercises to develop forethought: Visiting, and caring for, the plants and animals.

Note. From *The Montessori Method*, by Maria Montessori, 2012, p. 119.

However, contemporary Montessori practices often prioritize academic pursuits over outdoor play and Practical Life activities. Revisiting Montessori's emphasis on Practical Life exercises, the significance of conversation periods, and the role of the teacher as an observer and facilitator can enrich Montessori education and align it more closely with its original intentions. Furthermore, in Dr. Montessori's original schedule of the day, the importance of different types of play and outdoor experiences constitute the entire afternoon schedule. Children, according to Montessori's schedule of the day, spend time engaged in free play, directed play, and experiences in nature, all of which align with the suggestions from the American Academy of Pediatrics recommendation:

> Play and stress are closely linked. High amounts of play are associated with low levels of cortisol, suggesting either that play reduces stress or that unstressed animals play more. Play also activates norepinephrine, which facilitates learning at synapses and improves brain plasticity. Play, especially when accompanied by nurturing caregiving, may indirectly affect brain functioning by modulating or buffering adversity and by reducing toxic stress to levels that are more compatible with coping and resilience. (Yogman et al., 2018, pp. 5-6)

Many, if not most, Montessori schools and teacher preparation programs follow a dogmatic approach to the school day, focusing on academics. Now more than ever, children need the benefits of conversation with adults, hands-on purposeful activities, free play, directed play, and a connection with nature. Our observations must be of a free child. Current research shows the elements listed above are healthy and beneficial for child development—all are found in Montessori's original schedule (Chawla, 2015; Ginsburg et al., 2007). If the foundation of good practice is observation based on free activity in a prepared environment where children can move between indoor and outdoor activities as they please, we should return to that practice. Otherwise, we miss the conditions Montessori considered fundamental to be able to observe and the conditions necessary to allow for healing from the traumas of war, natural disasters, abuse, or tragedy.

The profound legacy of Dr. Maria Montessori as a scientist, educator, and activist beckons us to embrace a scientific pedagogy for a better world. Her commitment to understanding human development and fostering learning environments conducive to young children's growth and, ultimately, to a more peaceful world challenges us to take action.

In her speech at The Montessori Event 2024, Dr. Erica Moretti, author of *The Best Weapon for Peace* (2021), emphasized that Montessori's true mission was bringing about peace through education, that academic outcomes were an ancillary benefit to supporting children in becoming healthy, nourished humans who would prevent war. We agree with her and invite you to revisit and immerse yourself in the purposes of Montessori's scientific pedagogy, including the prepared environment, meaningful observation, and work with children experiencing trauma. In doing so, we can advocate for Montessori's place in our contemporary culture. As educators, we must break free from dogmatic approaches and embrace Montessori's original intentions, fostering environments where children can explore, learn, and grow. In doing so, we can work to continually grow in our embodiment of the spirit of Montessori's scientific pedagogy and pave the way for a more just, compassionate, and peaceful society.

Discussion Questions

- What biases or other internal barriers might prevent you from truly observing as Montessori intended?

- How might you commit to constantly evaluating and challenging existing norms and systems and asking yourself tough questions about the impact of the Montessori curriculum, pedagogy, and classroom environment on fostering critical thought, understanding, and empathy?

- What changes could you make to your environment to allow children to "be the master of [their] own force of will"?

References

Chawla, L. (2015). Benefits of nature contact for children. *Journal of Planning Literature, 30*(4), 433-452. https://doi.org/10.1177/0885412215595441

Ginsburg, K. R., & Committee on Psychosocial Aspects of Child and Family Health. (2007). The importance of play in promoting healthy child development and maintaining strong parent-child bonds. *Pediatrics, 119*(1), 182-191.

Kramer, R. (1976). *Maria Montessori : A biography.* Putnam.

Lyons-Ruth, K., Todd Manly, J., Von Klitzing, K., Tamminen, T., Emde, R., Fitzgerald, H., Paul,

C., Keren, M., Berg, A., Foley, M., & Watanabe, H. (2017). The worldwide burden of infant mental and emotional disorder: Report of the task force of the World Association for Infant Mental Health. *Infant Mental Health Journal, 38*(6), 695-705.

Montessori, M. (2016). Lecture 3: Some suggestions and remarks upon observing children. *The NAMTA Journal, 41*(3), 391–397.

Montessori, M. (2012). *The Montessori method.* Project Gutenberg. https://www.gutenberg.org/ebooks/39863

Montessori, M. (1995a). *The advanced Montessori method.* Thoemmes Press.

Montessori, M. (1995b). *The absorbent mind* (1st ed.). Henry Holt.

Montessori, M. (1992). *Education and peace.* Clio Press.

Montessori, M. (1967). *The discovery of the child.* Fides Publishers.

Montessori, M. (1966). *The secret of childhood.* Fides Publishers.

Montessori, M. (1917a). *The white cross.* AMI Journal 2013. Retrieved https://montessori.org.au/sites/default/files/downloads/publications/AMIJournalPreviewDec2013.pdf

Montessori, M. (1917b). *The advanced Montessori Method: Spontaneous activity in education.* Frederick A. Stokes Company.

Moretti, E. (2021). *The best weapon for peace: Maria Montessori, education, and children's rights.* University of Wisconsin Press

Montessori, M., & Haines, A. M., & Association Montessori Internationale (AMI). (2012). *The 1946 London lectures.* Montessori-Pierson Publishing.

Sackett, G. (2016). The scientist in the classroom: The Montessori teacher as scientist. *NAMTA Journal, 41*(2), 5-20.

Yogman, M., Garner, A., Hutchinson, J., Hirsh-Pasek, K., Golinkoff, R. M., Baum, R., Gambon,

T., Lavin, A., Mattson, G., Wissow, L., Hill, D. L., Ameenuddin, N., Chassiakos, Y. R., Cross, C., Boyd, R., Mendelson, R., Moreno, M. A., Radesky, J., Swanson, W. S. M., Hutchinsons, J., & Smith, J. (2018). The power of play: A pediatric role in enhancing development in young children. *Pediatrics, 142*(3). https://doi.org/10.1542/peds.2018-2058

CHAPTER 3

Innovation and Adaptation in the Montessori Prepared Environment

By Teresa Ripple, EdD, Allison Jones, MEd, and Olivia Christensen, PhD

What is a prepared Montessori environment? Montessori (2012) described "the adult, the child, and the environment [as] a trinity. They should be considered as one" (p. 213). The use of the word *trinity* evokes the sense of spiritual importance that Montessori attributed to these elements. Also called a triad, or triangle, this "trinity" consists of the physical (including the material), social, and cultural environment as prepared by the adult (the trained teacher) to provide a developmentally appropriate setting for the child. The prepared setting also includes the time, space, and materials that allow children to develop according to their nature (Lillard & McHugh, 2019, p. 4). Montessori (1967) made clear that the teacher's task, after preparing the environment, was to connect the child to the materials and leave the child free to work and develop. However, Montessori also indicated that "we can only help man if we aid the child to be better adapted to the future of civilization" (2012, p. 102). This paper explores how Montessori practitioners[1] can help children adapt to evolving societies, cultures, and languages by asking themselves the following questions: Are there aspects of the Montessori environment that need adaptation or innovation to

---

1 We use the term *practitioners* to include all professionals in the Montessori environment.

serve children today? How do we stay authentic to Montessori's ideas and theories while considering current research and contemporary educational theories? Finally, how do we empower Montessori practitioners to best meet the needs of all children in the environment?

Montessori Was a Person of Her Time and Place

Montessori's writing and pedagogy reflect who she was as a Catholic woman living in Italy in the late 19th and early 20th century. The children in Montessori's first Children's House came from the same cultural, ethnic, and likely the same religious background as the practitioners. This context influenced how Montessori designed her Method, yet that context is dissimilar from many of our communities and schools today. While the principles of Montessori pedagogy are sound and upheld by current research,[2] social context influences how those principles are applied throughout the environment and instruction. For example, Montessori designed a language and literacy curriculum based on her own Italian language, which is largely phonetic. However, in the United States, the language curriculum contains materials different from the original Italian curriculum because of the complexity of English. Adapting the original Montessori language materials was necessary to meet the needs of a predominantly English-speaking culture. By contrast, many Early Childhood classrooms today still contain silver polishing, although it is not an activity of Practical Life in most children's homes the way it was in 19th-century Italy. It is crucial for Montessori practitioners to adapt Practical Life materials to reflect the communities and culture served in classrooms, similar to the adaptations made in the Language curriculum.

Montessori teacher education, frequently referred to as "teacher training," provides content in a way that suggests practitioners replicate their training in their future classroom environment, just as Montessori described in her writings

---

2 See Lillard and McHugh, 2019, page 2 for an extensive list of the research studying the efficacy of Montessori education.

and lectures. While preserving authenticity, this pedagogical training may inhibit practitioners from implementing innovative ideas relevant to current culture and communities (Chapter 9 discusses Montessori teacher education at length). Lillard and McHugh described "authentic" Montessori as implemented in the traditional or original way, using the word *authentic* as defined by the Oxford Dictionary , but also noted that "Dr.

> Just as Montessori adjusted her work to accommodate children's differing needs in her time, today's practitioners can make effective and culturally relevant adjustments to their practices in serving the diverse needs of children in today's Montessori classrooms.

Montessori adjusted approaches in response to children's developmental needs based on her observations. Had she lived longer, her ideas would surely have evolved" (2019, p. 2). Just as Montessori adjusted her work to accommodate children's differing needs in her time, today's practitioners can make effective and culturally relevant adjustments to their practices in serving the diverse needs of children in today's Montessori classrooms.

Three modern-day lenses that may provide practitioners a framework are 1) culturally sustaining pedagogy, 2) Universal Design for Learning, and 3) family and community partnerships. To apply these lenses, shared definitions are necessary.

Culturally Sustaining Pedagogy

Ladson-Billings created the term *culturally relevant pedagogy* to describe a "theoretical model that not only addresses student achievement but also helps students to accept and affirm their cultural identity while developing critical perspectives that challenge inequities that schools (and other institutions) perpetuate" (1995, p. 469). Practitioners who enact culturally relevant pedagogy believe that students of all racial, ethnic, and cultural backgrounds can achieve academically, and that students have numerous ways to demonstrate competence; they work to empower students and build on their strengths while holding them to high standards (Mensah, 2021). *Culturally sustaining pedagogy,* an alternative term coined by Paris (2012), describes how teaching practice can go beyond being "relevant" or "responsive" to sustaining and fostering "linguistic, literate, and cultural pluralism" in schools (pp. 93–97). See Chapters 7, 8, and 9 for a deeper dive into culturally relevant and sustaining pedagogy.

Universal Design for Learning

Montessori wrote extensively on the repressive experiences children had, which stifled their independence, and creativity, and ultimately prevented them from reaching their true potential (Montessori, 1991, 1972, 2008). As such, she developed her method of education to not only better support early childhood development, but also to offer children reprieve from an oppressive society. Montessori explained:

> A more just and charitable approach towards the child would be to create an "adaptive" environment different from the repressive one in which he operates and which has already formed his character. The implementation of any educational system ought to begin with the creation of an environment that protects the child from the difficult and dangerous obstacles that threaten him in the adult world. (Montessori, 1946/1991, p. 5)

The concept of an adaptive, inclusive environment that addresses the unique needs of the child by minimizing detrimental difficulties aligns with a key component of Universal Design for Learning (IDA, 2021).

Universal Design for Learning (UDL) is an educational framework based on research in cognitive neuroscience to design learning spaces that address the diverse needs of learners (Rose, 2000). UDL expands on the concept of inclusion, or providing access to learning for students with disabilities through accommodations and modifications, to suggest that the initial design of learning environments should meet a diversity of learning styles and needs. The three principles of UDL are multiple means of representation, multiple means of expression, and multiple means of engagement (Orkwis & McLane, 1998). UDL aims to ensure that all learners can access and participate in meaningful, challenging learning opportunities by reducing physical, cognitive, intellectual, and organizational barriers (CAST, 2018).

Family and Community Partnership

Research has demonstrated that thoughtful family engagement correlates to improved student outcomes (Kelty & Wakabayashi, 2020). However, Montessori practitioners sometimes struggle to create genuine opportunities for families to engage meaningfully with their child's development and co-construct curriculum, possibly due to the specificity and complexity of the Montessori curriculum (you can read more about this in Chapter 8). A review of Montessori school websites found in a Google search suggested that common strategies for family engagement include inviting caregivers to observe in the classroom, and providing opportunities for families to understand the Montessori method and implement it in the home environment. Strategies for including families in the preparation of the prepared environment and in the creation of culturally sustaining materials were not widely featured. Family partnership is a prerequisite to creating prepared environments that reflect children's identity and community, and are designed to meet their individual needs. Families provide key expertise on their child's strengths and their community's cultural characteristics, both of which are needed to enact culturally sustaining pedagogy and Universal Design for Learning.

Applying the concepts of culturally sustaining practices, Universal Design for Learning, and family and community partnerships to the prepared environment provides a framework for innovation and adaptation that supports Montessori pedagogy and ensures it continues to meet the needs of all children. The essential component for successful integration of these elements in the environment is the adult. The next sections will demonstrate innovative approaches and adaptations to the Montessori physical/material environment and the social/cultural environment.

The Material/Physical Environment

To meet the needs of all children in the physical environment, the practitioner must begin by assessing the physical environment to ensure it provides access to learning for all students and reflects the cultures of the classroom community. In Montessori classrooms, some key areas to assess are the charts used in Elementary classrooms to illustrate and explain botany, biology, and geography concepts, the books that are available, and the geography and history curricula. Charts such as the "people of different zones" that portray overly stereotypical images of people from different continents should be removed or replaced with inclusive versions. Books should include and feature people of different genders, races, religions, abilities, and backgrounds, with special attention to removing those with stereotypical associations. Materials in the geography and history curricula are especially vulnerable to Eurocentric, stereotypical imagery. For example, the geography folders in Early Childhood classrooms can easily espouse a "tourist curriculum" that depicts non-European cultures as exotic and limited in scope. The puzzle maps promote a Eurocentric point of view,[3] as they reflect the Mercator projection that depicts Europe and North America as disproportionately large, while countries in Africa and South America are disproportionately small (Richards, Cooley, Miller, and Watterson, 2024). Similarly, the history curriculum in Elementary classrooms can be overfocused on European civilizations and European history.

The practitioner must ensure that all children have physical and intellectual access to learning. This can look like physical changes to typical Montessori materials, such as providing non-sandpaper letters for a child with sensory sensitivities, or adaptive seating for children with limited core strength. Access can also include accommodations or adaptations that support children's understanding within a lesson or during independent practice, such as providing visual aids or creating additional lessons to bolster a student's missing skills.

---

3 See https://sites.lsa.umich.edu/qmss/2022/06/14
why-your-view-of-the-world-may-be-completely-wrong/

Lillard and McHugh (2019) also include within the prepared environment the "temporal environment" (p. 8) which encompasses a 3-hour work cycle. This breadth of time is thought to allow children to naturally develop in relationship with both the material and social environment, without interruption. During this period, children choose activities and work independently, developing concentration and self-discipline in concert with the materials and the other children. By contrast, a recent study found that Maria Montessori herself did not adhere to a strict 3-hour work cycle, but scheduled various activities throughout a 2.5-hour period (Morgan Herman, 2023). Regardless, the strict schedule to which some schools adhere may not align with children's home culture and temporal rhythms, and restrict parent and child access when the hours and activities are not reflective of the family's home and work responsibilities.

The Social/Cultural Environment

The social component of the prepared environment includes the child and the other children in the 3-year age cycle, as well as any other adults who interact with the child in the classroom environment. The limited quantity of materials the children encounter and the lessons in Grace and Courtesy support the development of prosocial skills such as collaboration and taking turns. The procedures, routines, and Grace and Courtesy lessons are most effectively designed to build bridges to and from children's home culture and ways of interacting outside the classroom. Hammond (2015) explains:

> Culture, it turns out, is the way that every brain makes sense of the world. This is why everyone, regardless of race or ethnicity, has a culture. Think of culture as software for the brain's hardware. The brain uses cultural information to turn everyday happenings into meaningful events. (p. 22)

Children use their everyday lived experience, or "funds of knowledge,"[4] to make sense of the world, especially in learning new ideas. Building on their

---

4 See Vélez-Ibáñez, C.G., and Greenberg, J.B. (1992) for original source of the term.

existing skills, knowledge, and experiences, whether that is knowing that eye contact with adults is not culturally appropriate at home or creating lessons that reflect forms of greeting used in their own communities, both honors children's home culture and creates opportunities for them to learn to interact in cultures that are not their own.

Ensuring that the social environment is culturally sustaining requires thoughtful work by the practitioner. Iruku, Curenton, Durden, and Escayg (2020) affirmed that when "culturally affirming" practices are used in the environment, children see themselves as "cultural leaders," and opportunity gaps between white students and black students are decreased (p. 60). To ensure that a practitioner builds a culturally affirming environment, reflection "on learned personal ideas and beliefs surrounding race, ethnicity, culture, and identities" is necessary (Norris, 2023, p. 28). Because the prepared classroom environment "outwardly mirrors... internal beliefs, worldviews, and racial attitudes" (Iruku et al., 2023, p. 46), Montessori practitioners must interrogate their instructional practices from a culturally sustaining point of view, and determine if a white or Eurocentric identity is being upheld in the environments (Iruku et al., 2023, p. 55). Personal culture and experiences implicitly and explicitly influence which Practical Life exercises to put on the shelves, or how to design a Grace and Courtesy lesson. Unlike Montessori's monocultural classroom in Italy, the children in our schools likely reflect multiple intersectional identities and potentially multiple linguistic backgrounds. Classrooms today must reflect a wide array of cultural identities to foster a sense of belonging for all students. For example, books that feature a diversity of characters and lifestyles not only help children see themselves as part of the classroom community, but also introduce others to the vast diversity of the world. Classroom art and other imagery can have the same effect and foster a sense of belonging. Practitioners should also think about the activities of Practical Life, including Grace and Courtesy lessons, to ensure they are inclusive of a variety of ways of living and forms of social interactions. Montessori could not anticipate many of the experiences children face today, nor did she describe ways to address microaggressions[5] that may happen in the classroom, or refer to the cultural environment, particularly at the early childhood level. Rather, Montessori (2008) described characteristics of a successful school environment such as: "these children adapt easily to everything, to work and to contact with others" (p. 22). Today, we know there is much to consider regarding a child's adaptation to a new environment, ranging from personal and family identities and home culture to the effects of trauma. Not only do practitioners need to consider how they can support and connect with each unique child, but they should also be aware of how broader social patterns infiltrate classroom experiences, both implicitly and explicitly, marginalizing and privileging certain ways of being.

It is worth noting that Dr. Montessori died in 1952 in Amsterdam, 2 years before the lengthy process of desegregating American schools began. Furthermore, the majority of her work with children occurred in relatively homogenous countries–Italy and India. While she championed the education of children in poverty and children with learning disabilities of her time, the school communities in which she worked were typically culturally and racially uniform. Social adaptation then was different than it is now and Montessori admonished us that "we can only help man if we aid the child to be better adapted to the future of civilization" (2012, p. 102).

Making Decisions about What to Implement

In a classroom of 20 to 35 children with different cultural backgrounds and unique physical, learning, and developmental needs, it can be overwhelming to determine what to implement in the prepared environment while adhering to the principles of Montessori education. Part of the strength of Montessori is that there are a wide variety of practices that can be used to meet children's

---

5 Racial microaggressions are "daily verbal, behavioral, or environmental indignities, whether intentional or unintentional, that communicate hostile, derogatory, or negative racial slights and insults toward people of color" (Sue et al, 2007). Microaggressions can also happen for other identity markers such as sexual orientation, gender identity, class, nationality, etc.

needs. Part of the challenge is freeing Montessori practitioners from the idea that accommodation is straying from authentic Montessori practice. Six key framing questions can help practitioners determine whether or not to add to or adapt their prepared environment.

Intentional selection of materials: Does an existing material in the classroom meet the need?

In one study, children in high-fidelity Montessori classrooms, defined as Montessori classrooms without extensive supplemental materials, showed significantly greater gains in measures of executive function, reading, math, vocabulary, and social problem-solving (Lillard, 2012). Because of the efficacy of the Montessori materials, when considering adding new materials, we should first ask, is there an existing material in the classroom that meets this need? For example, if a child needs additional work with fine motor skills, the existing Practical Life activities may be sufficient. However, if a child needs support remembering the steps to the Stamp Game, the teacher may consider adding a needed visual aid to guide the child as an extension of the activity.

Universal Design for Learning: Is the adaptation specific to one child, or would it benefit all children?

Adaptations, or accommodations, can be helpful when they meet the needs of the children who need them, as in the example above, providing a visual aid to a child who needs support remembering the steps of the Stamp Game. However, they can be harmful when incorrectly applied, and an accommodation helpful to one child may not be helpful to all (Kagan et al., 2017). For example, just because one child needs a visual aid for the Stamp Game doesn't mean all the children in the classroom do. Conversely, some adaptations are, in fact, helpful for all children (Cahan et al., 2016). For example, having headphones or lap weights available for all children to use when they need them is Universal Design for Learning.

Control of error: **Does the addition or adaptation require high adult support?**

Many strategies used in intervention depend on a high level of adult support. For example, a lesson on syllabication with the Movable Alphabet might be very helpful for a child struggling with decoding. However, if it required the practitioner to sit by the child and direct every step of the child's work, it would not be sustainable. Montessori classrooms rely on children being able to independently engage with practice after a presentation, so any addition or adaptation should be designed to require the least adult support possible.

Choice: **Does the material preserve child choice?**

Any addition or adaptation should preserve children's ability to choose their work, interact with it until they feel completion, and then put it away. For example, a child who is struggling with making independent choices may benefit from limited choices laid out on a choice board, to help them learn to choose from a smaller set of options before taking on choosing from the entire classroom. However, if that choice board lays out only practitioner-selected activities that the child must do in a certain order, it does not build their ability to choose.

Independence: **Is the addition or adaptation designed to build children's skills?**

Any accommodation, addition, or adaptation should be designed to build the child's skills so that eventually it will no longer be needed. This is called "fading"—or gradually decreasing the amount of support as a child gains skill until they can function independently (Estrapala et al., 2018). For example, if a child struggles with certain steps of a complex Practical Life activity, creating additional preliminary activities to build that skill can build independence until those preliminary steps are no longer needed. Conversely, having a peer complete that step for them, or changing the activity so that the step is irrelevant does not build skill and independence. A clear exception is physical accommodations. For example, if a child needs larger print because they have limited sight, or larger tray handles because of a physical difference, fading does not apply.

Interdependence: **Does this addition or adaptation support children's inter-dependence as part of the classroom community?**

In *Discovery of the Child,* Montessori describes how "through practical exercises...the children develop a true "social feeling," for they are working in the environment of the community in which they live, without concerning themselves as to whether it is for their own, or for the common good" (1967, p. 97). Any addition, adaptation, or accommodation should support children's integration into and contribution to the classroom community. For example, individual seating or self-regulation spaces allow children to choose when to interact with the community and when they need time alone. Grace and Courtesy lessons about the use of those spaces allow children the opportunity to build up their understanding of and respect for others' social-emotional needs. Conversely, assigned individualized seating separates a child from their community, and does not build the social skills or impulse control that they need in order to function interdependently.

Conclusion

Montessori believed that the prepared environment "itself will teach the child, if every error [they make] is manifest to [them], without the intervention of parent or practitioner, who should remain a quiet observer of all that happens" (Montessori, 1989, p. 28). While the practitioner may be a "quiet observer," the preparation required to build and maintain a culturally responsive prepared environment that reflects the identities of the children who learn there is vast. The lenses of culturally sustaining practices, UDL, and family/community partnership provide an initial framework for this practice.

Discussion Questions

- How can you interrogate your instructional practices from a culturally sustaining point of view to determine if a white or Eurocentric identity is being upheld in your environment?

- "Part of the strength of Montessori is that there are a wide variety of practices that can be used to meet children's needs. Part of the challenge is freeing Montessori practitioners from the idea that accommodation is straying from authentic Montessori practice."

Spend some time reflecting on these two statements. What comes up when you consider adapting Montessori materials and pedagogy? What do you need, if anything, to be free from the idea that accommodation is straying from authentic Montessori practice?

- Review the six framing questions and consider whether or not adaptation is needed in your environment.

References

Cahan, S., Nirel, R., & Alkoby, M. (2016). The extra-examination time granting policy: A reconceptualization. *Journal of Psychoeducational Assessment, 34*(5), 461–472. doi:10.1177/0734282915616537

CAST. (2018). *Universal design for learning guidelines version 2.2.* Retrieved from http://udlguidelines.cast.org

Costa, S., Pirchio, S., Shevchuk, A., & Glock, S. (2023). Does teachers' ethnic bias stress them out? The role of teachers' implicit attitudes toward and expectations of ethnic minority students in teachers' burnout. *International Journal of Intercultural Relations, 93,*(101757), 1–11. https://doi.org/10.1016/j.ijintrel.2023.101757

Estrapala, S., Rila, A., & Bruhn, A. L. (2018). Don't quit cold turkey: Systematic fading to promote sustained behavioral change. *Teaching Exceptional Children, 51*(1), 54–61. https://doi.org/10.1177/0040059918790567

Hammond, Z. L. (2015). *Culturally responsive teaching and the brain.* Corwin Press.

International Disability Alliance (IDA). (2021). Universal design for learning and its role in ensuring access to inclusive education for all. Retrieved from https://www.internationaldisabilityalliance.org/sites/default/files/universal_design_for_learning_final_8.09.2021.pdf

Iruka, I. U., Curenton, S. M., Durden, T. R., & Escayg, K. A. (2020). *Don't look away: Embracing anti-bias classrooms.* Gryphon House.

Kelty, N. E., & Wakabayashi, T. (2020). Family engagement in schools: Parent, educator, and community perspectives. *SAGE Open, 10*(4). https://doi.org/10.1177/2158244020973024

Lillard, A. (2012). Preschool children's development in classic Montessori, supplemented

Montessori, and conventional programs. *Journal of School Psychology, 50*(3), 379–401. https://doi.org/10.1016/j.jsp.2012.01.001.

Lillard, A., & McHugh, V. (2019). Authentic Montessori: The Dottoressa's view at the end of her life part I: The environment. *Journal of Montessori Research, 5*(1). 1–18.

Kagan, E. R., Frank, H. E., & Kendall, P. C. (2017). Accommodation in youth with OCD and anxiety. *Clinical Psychology: Science and Practice, 24*(1), 78–98. https://doi.org/10.1111/cpsp.12186

Ladson-Billings, G. (1995). But that's just good teaching! The case for culturally relevant pedagogy. *Theory Into Practice 34*(3), 469.

Mensah, F. M. (2021). Culturally relevant and culturally responsive: Two theories of practice for science teaching. *Science and Children, 58*(4). https://www.nsta.org/science-and-children/science-and-children-marchapril-2021/culturally-relevant-and-culturally

Montessori, M. (1991). *Education for a new world.* Kalakshetra Press. (Original published work 1946)

Montessori, M. (1972). *The discovery of the child.* Ballantine Books. (Original published work 1967)

Montessori, M. (2008). *The child, society and the world. Unpublished speeches and writings.* Montessori-Pierson Publishing.

Montessori, M. (2012). *The 1946 London lectures.* Montessori-Pierson Publishing.

Montessori, M. (1989). *The child in the family.* Clio Press.

Morgan Herman, J. (2023). Mandate or myth? The uninterrupted 3-hour work cycle. *Montessori Life, 35*(1), 46–49.

Orkwis, R., & McLane, K. (1998). *A curriculum every student can use: Design principles for student access.* [Topical Brief] ERIC/OSEP Special Project. Retrieved from https://eric.ed.gov/?id=ED423654

Paris, D. (2012). Culturally sustaining pedagogy: A needed change in stance, terminology, and practice. *Educational Researcher 41*(3), 93–97. https://doi.org/10.3102/0013189X12441244

Richards, A. S., Cooley, E., Miller, J., & Watterson, R. (2024). Testing the Mercator effect: Global map projections persuade differently according to the emphasis frames used to contextualize them. *Communication Reports, 37*(2), 109–123.

Rose, D. (2000). Universal design for learning. *Journal of Special Education Technology, 15*(4), 47–51. https://doi.org/10.1177/016264340001500407

Sue, D. W., Capodilupo, C. M., Torino, G. C., Bucceri, J. M., Holder, A. M., Nadal, K. L., & Esquilin, M. (2007). Racial microaggressions in everyday life: Implications for clinical practice. *American Psychologist. 62*(4):271–86. https://doi.org/10.1037/0003-066X.62.4.271

Vélez-Ibáñez, C. G., & Greenberg, J.B. (1992). Formation and transformation of funds of knowledge among U.S. Mexican households. *Anthropology & Education Quarterly, 23*(4), 313–335.

CHAPTER 4

Access and Full Implementation: Challenges and Opportunities in Public Montessori

By Genevieve D'Cruz, PhD, and Elizabeth Slade, MFA

To bring a complete perspective to the topic of Montessori in public schools in the United States, it's important to understand the history of the Method's arrival. Soon after the first Montessori schools opened in the United States in 1911 and 1912, conflict arose between Montessori's wish to maintain the purity of the Method and her American supporters' wish for widespread dispersion of the Method (Whitescarver & Cossentino, 2008). The tension between the desire to reach all children (to replicate quickly, shorten the length of training, and supplement materials) and the wish to maintain the integrity of the Method (beginning with one age group and building on each year, training teachers full-time for a year, and purchasing materials from authorized vendors who use particular blueprints) has continued in the Montessori community for decades. It provides an overarching lens for this chapter, in which we will outline the challenges and opportunities of practicing Montessori in public settings.

As two long-standing public Montessori educators, we come to the topic of public Montessori with a deep commitment to the Montessori Method and providing access for all children. Our work as public Montessori practitioners has guided our perspectives on challenges and opportunities in public Montessori education. In this chapter, we closely examine the public-sector challenges in access to and full implementation of Montessori. We then discuss the opportunities the public sector allows us in the areas mentioned earlier and share recommendations for taking advantage of these opportunities to enact fully implemented, accessible Montessori programs. To interpret and address the challenges and opportunities we discuss, we use the **Critical Montessori Model (CMM).** This theoretical model assumes high-fidelity Montessori practice and is built on a foundation of **critical race theory** (D'Cruz, 2022). The CMM draws from theories such as **community cultural wealth, culturally sustaining pedagogy**, and **counter-storytelling** to take a strengths-based approach (also inherent to the Montessori Method) and an anti-racist lens to identify challenges and opportunities and to make recommendations to strengthen how Montessori is practiced. While critical race theory assumes a permanence of racism, interwoven into the systems and structures in the United States, theories such as community cultural wealth, culturally sustaining pedagogy, and counter-storytelling offer paths forward in anti-racist, anti-bias education.

Challenges to Public Montessori

Access

While there are challenges in enacting Montessori in any context, due to variations in training, interpretation, and practice, the public setting presents unique challenges to the Method. One such challenge is the limited access to Montessori programs, both physically and relationally, particularly for BIPOC (Black, Indigenous, People of Color) communities. By "physically," we refer to the racially representative and geographical makeup of public Montessori schools. While public Montessori school students are more likely than their conventional-school counterparts to attend racially diverse schools, not all public Montessori schools boast racial diversity; in fact, there are fewer BIPOC students and families in public Montessori schools than their surrounding districts (Debs, 2016). With limited access to public Montessori education comes limited literature and research about public Montessori; much of the existing research primarily reflects white students and families (Educational Testing Service, 2019). By "relational" access, we mean how students experience the Method. In the way it is practiced, Montessori is specifically inaccessible to BIPOC communities; public Montessori schools are no exception (D'Cruz, 2023). Children of different racial groups experience Montessori differently (Ansari & Winsler, 2014). Without interpretation through a critical racial lens, BIPOC Montessori educators and students may struggle to relate to the philosophy in the way it is enacted through lessons (D'Cruz, 2023). For example, many Primary Montessori teacher education programs encourage educators to change their way of speaking to enunciate more, claiming that children will write what they hear, and that saying each letter or sound of each word will help children in their writing progress. While this may be true, asking educators to change their speech and language style leads to an erasure of elements of educator identities (D'Cruz, 2023).

Using a critical racial lens involves acknowledging the ways that white supremacy is baked into the structures of the United States (Ladson-Billings, 1998). White supremacy and racism are ordinary (not irregular) in U.S. society; this makes it difficult to address them because they often go unacknowledged (Delgado & Stefancic, 2017). While obvious forms of discrimination, such as redlining, stand out, other systemic inequities present themselves more subtly. For example, assessments have historically shown that Black children perform worse than white children (Ladson-Billings, 1998). As Montessori in the United States exists in a white supremacist educational system, it is essential to recognize and uplift BIPOC students' strengths and capabilities to actively practice it in an anti-racist way.[6] Explicitly supporting BIPOC students is one way to counteract the racist systems and structures that surround all of us in the United States.

---

6 Because BIPOC individuals have historically been oppressed, for Montessori to truly reach "all children," we must specifically name those who have been historically excluded and encountered barriers to accessing Montessori education; a framework of critical race theory allows us to specifically center those who have been excluded due to race. While, for the purposes of this chapter, we frequently use the term "all children," we simultaneously recognize the importance of explicitly naming BIPOC students as they have been historically excluded from educational opportunities. By using the CMM to guide this chapter and our recommendations, we hope to move away from the use of such terms as performative, and instead move toward action.

Full Implementation

Montessori implementation can vary widely depending on leader and educator preparation, as it is not a trademarked approach. Montessori teacher education varies in format (i.e., in-person versus online), time commitment (full-time versus part-time), requirements (such as practice teaching, observation), art of teaching (such as classroom leadership), and inclusion of ABAR (anti-bias, anti-racist) principles. Thus, teachers emerge from training with a wide range of preparation for the experience of leading a classroom with three age groups, which in public schools translates to three grades of standards. When implemented fully, Montessori education is a viable choice for BIPOC students, specifically Black students, but not all schools implement Montessori fully (Jor'dan, 2017). Full implementation means every classroom has a Montessori-trained teacher, a 3-year age span, and an uninterrupted work cycle, as well as core elements of the Method, including full sets of Montessori materials, freedom of choice, and consistent standards of practice (Jor'dan, 2017). The decisions made in public Montessori schools often perpetuate the inequities seen in conventional schools. Those involved in decision-making for public Montessori do not always fully understand its benefits; many schools use enrichment programs and high-stakes achievement testing and reflect inequitable resources and opportunities in conventional U.S. public schools (Chattin-McNichols, 2016). Without ways to compare data, public Montessori schools are often forced to use existing and conventional assessments, behavior management systems, and additional enrichment programs to appear comparable to their traditional counterparts, thus also facing the pitfalls of perpetuating inequity for their BIPOC students through practices proven to set up BIPOC students for failure (Rosales & Walker, 2021).

A related challenge to fully implementing the Method in public Montessori schools is curriculum alignment and standards. Montessori cannot always be compared with conventional methods, often due to its varying implementation (Lillard, 2019). Due to its scope and sequence, it is not always a direct comparison. For example, Montessori students in their first-grade year learn equivalent fractions. Students in conventional classrooms do not learn about fractions until they are in the third grade.[7] Additionally, Montessori students use didactic materials to understand math concepts and do not always move to abstraction until third grade, whereas conventional students learn math concepts abstractly from the start. While this may not need to present a challenge in the day-to-day operations of a Montessori classroom, public Montessori school teachers are held to the same expectations as conventional teachers and are expected to deliver similar academic outcomes, despite there being an established Montessori scope and sequence that is often out of step with their district mandates. As a result, some programs elect to use only the section of the vast Montessori curriculum that aligns with district expectations, thus not fully implementing the model.

While numerous other challenges face public Montessori schools, we highlight the above dilemmas to open up a discussion of the opportunities to address these challenges through systemic and individual decisions, practices, and interpretations. In the following section, we discuss the possibilities that arise when we frame these challenges as opportunities and share our recommendations for increasing access and strengthening fully implemented Montessori in the public sector.

Opportunities for Public Montessori

Access: Interpretation and Practice

While physical access is still a challenge, the public Montessori community has also successfully brought together students from various racial and socioeconomic backgrounds (Debs, 2016). As mentioned earlier, the Critical Montessori Model provides a framework and lens for educators to acknowledge the barriers that BIPOC students and educators face while uplifting their lived experiences. The Critical Montessori Model assumes that Montessori must be practiced with a critical racial lens; to do this, the model draws on culturally sustaining pedagogy, community cultural wealth, and counter-storytelling. Educators

---

7 See Common Core State Standards (thecorestandards.org)

interested in using the CMM must first acknowledge the white supremacist structures inherent in the United States.[8] Then, using a strengths-based lens, they can examine and understand their students' experiences and identify their strengths (which can take many forms, such as linguistic abilities or the support they receive from their social and community networks). BIPOC Montessori educators can also use the model similarly; first, they can examine their lived experiences and strengths and then determine how to bring those into the classroom space. One example of this is a Black Montessori educator who, upon reflecting on her relationship and experience with her hair, wrote a lesson to share with students about the varying textures, styles, and care of different hair types (D'Cruz, 2023). In the following paragraphs, we explain how theories can be implemented to support BIPOC Montessori community members explicitly.

Schools have the opportunity to be proactive in recruiting BIPOC students and families; one way to do this is to increase the amount of BIPOC Montessori teaching staff (Debs & Brown, 2017). To do so, Montessori teacher training and public Montessori schools could weave **culturally sustaining pedagogy** into their methods and give adults the opportunities and time to do the internal work needed to support their students (Brown & Steele, 2015; D'Cruz, 2022). Culturally sustaining pedagogy invites educators to not only acknowledge students' identities and experiences but to also actively uplift and sustain their cultures. This could look like creating new anti-bias, anti-racist lessons to share with students (which many Montessori schools are already doing), or reexamining existing systems or expectations in schools. For example, enacting culturally sustaining pedagogy for multilingual learners could look like inviting students to bring their own language knowledge into the classroom to support their learning or to pair or group students who speak the same home language

---

8 For example, in an educational setting, school curricula have historically been used to uphold white supremacy by centering white dominant male perspectives as the standard of knowledge (Ladson-Billings, 1998). This means that BIPOC voices are erased. This is an active process that is currently happening in states such as Florida that are banning or restricting how or whether Black history, in particular, is taught. Such restrictions erase the full experiences of Black individuals and the history of enslavement in the United States (Najarro, 2023).

to encourage them to engage with content in their home languages. In planning Grace and Courtesy lessons in the Early Childhood classroom, educators could reach out to families before the beginning of the school year to ask what they want their children to be able to know and do. Part of the work required when increasing opportunities for access means intentionally using a strengths-based lens rather than a deficit mindset when working with students.

Community cultural wealth (Yosso, 2005) offers a framework for educators to see their students' strengths outside academics alone. By acknowledging that students come into the classroom with strengths (or capital) such as linguistic abilities, knowing how to navigate oppressive systems, the strength and ability to use their actions as forms of resistance, strong family systems, and more, Montessori educators can use the Montessori Method to better highlight their students' strengths and abilities (D'Cruz, 2023). While varying interpretations of Montessori can make it challenging for individual BIPOC students to access the curriculum in the classroom, schools as a whole face institutional racism and need to foster cultural competency (Brown & Steele, 2015).

Another way to calibrate educators' interpretations and enactments of Montessori is through offering professional development in **professional learning communities (PLCs)** (Jones, 2020; Leonard & Woodland, 2022). Ongoing, consistent opportunities for staff to gather and reflect on their practice and how they interpret and enact the curriculum are necessary for anti-racist professional development to be effective (Leonard & Woodland, 2022). PLCs can offer opportunities for every educator in the school to be a member of a group that follows clearly defined processes to discuss how to enact anti-racist instructional practices (Woodland & Mazur, 2018). While time is limited in public schools, taking even 30 minutes a week has been linked to teachers' perceptions of higher-quality teaching practices (Woodland & Mazur, 2018). **Lesson study** is an excellent opportunity to take an existing process and use an equity lens to examine a lesson. This includes asking what assumptions we make about the lesson before we give it, or what we imagine the lesson should look like based on our training. We can incorporate a more critical lens into our practice by challenging our preconceived notions and questioning our assumptions.

The path to witnessing stories requires redefining power relationships in classrooms and in schools. To move from listening with judgment—when teachers assume power roles and fail to fully listen to the students—to listening with a sense of curiosity and determination to know differently requires that participants open their hearts and minds to diverse stories and a new way to teach.

Finally, **counter-storytelling** offers a way for BIPOC educators and students to share their experiences and disrupt dominant narratives, or to emphasize non-dominant narratives. In a classroom, this could look like a teacher challenging historical narratives typically told from a dominant perspective. In Montessori Elementary classrooms, where performances and speeches are common curriculum elements, students could be invited to share their counter-stories, while others practice fully listening (Machado, 2023). Machado (2023) describes witnessing as a form of deep listening:

> The path to witnessing stories requires redefining power relationships in classrooms and in schools. To move from listening with judgment—when teachers assume power roles and fail to fully listen to the students—to listening with a sense of curiosity and determination to know differently requires that participants open their hearts and minds to diverse stories and a new way to teach. (p. 85)

This deep listening means that, in counter-storytelling, hierarchy is disregarded, power dynamics are resisted, and the storyteller and listener are on the same level (Machado, 2023). An educator supporting counter-storytelling in their classroom listens to their students' stories without trying to correct, but rather to understand, a concept that lends itself well to the Montessori value of respect and reverence for the child.

Figure 1 provides a visual for the CMM and shows how various elements intertwine to provide a critical lens for the Montessori practitioner.

Figure 1

The Critical Montessori Model

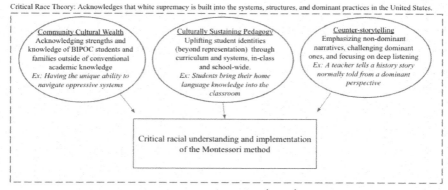

Critical Montessori Model

Core assumption: Montessori needs to be read, interpreted, and practiced through a critical racial perspective.

Critical Race Theory: Acknowledges that white supremacy is built into the systems, structures, and dominant practices in the United States.

Community Cultural Wealth
Acknowledging strengths and knowledge of BIPOC students and families outside of conventional academic knowledge
Ex: Having the unique ability to navigate oppressive systems

Culturally Sustaining Pedagogy
Uplifting student identities (beyond representation) through curriculum and systems, in-class and school-wide.
Ex: Students bring their home language knowledge into the classroom

Counter-storytelling
Emphasizing non-dominant narratives, challenging dominant ones, and focusing on deep listening
Ex: A teacher tells a history story normally told from a dominant perspective

Critical racial understanding and implementation of the Montessori method

Note. From D'Cruz, G. (2023)

Access: Policies and Systems

Another opportunity for public Montessori schools is to reexamine their institutional policies and practices to ensure that they are not perpetuating obstacles to access through racist practices. While individuals can do the work of self-reflection and use culturally sustaining instructional methods, supporting strong, anti-racist systems ensures that school as an institution will systematically increase access to Montessori. Schools can use other elements of the Critical Montessori Model to support inclusive policies and systems. In a school setting, administrators could invite BIPOC educators or families to share their counter-stories and use them to reflect on and help shape how educators and families relate to and experience school. Again, with storytellers and listeners on the same level, disregarding hierarchy and power, schools can co-create a school climate and systems that reflect and support their BIPOC educators and families. Using community cultural wealth, schools can shift practices to first center their communities' strengths. For example, a school might use the practice of first reaching out to current families for support when doing outreach to prospective families. Inviting existing families to bring their language abilities and community connections to events such as tours or open houses can create a system steeped in community.

Jones' (2020) analysis of anti-racist policies outlines five areas of focus to address racism in school: school environment, incident reporting, staffing, data analysis, and funding. Anti-racist school practices go beyond creating an equity-centered climate in classrooms and throughout the school. Most policies have reporting requirements for racial incidents and a specific procedure to follow. In a Montessori school, such a procedure could include a student conference, mediation, and strategies for dealing with racial conflict (at the Elementary level and above).

While public schools may not control which assessments they can offer and how much funding they receive, they can focus their hiring processes on recruiting and retaining staff with anti-racist mindsets and support them through PLCs as outlined above. Schools may also have control over their staff appraisals; appraisals that outline specific actions educators can take to support an anti-racist school climate are another way to support anti-racist practices within the school. When anti-racist actions become part of a school's policies and practices, they are no longer dependent on individuals, and can become a core part of the institution.

Access: Constructivist Approaches to Student Behavior

As part of interpreting students' abilities through a strengths-based lens, public Montessori schools can develop a strong system of justness by implementing a constructivist behavior management system in response to students (Slade, 2021). Conventional behaviorist systems see a disproportionate number of BIPOC students out of the classroom for "discipline" issues, thus limiting their access to a Montessori education; even in Montessori schools, Black and Brown students have been shown to spend more time out of school than their white counterparts, a phenomenon known as racial discipline disproportionality (Brown & Steele, 2015). Rather than a conventional system of discipline, Montessori schools can use the **Nautilus Approach,** which follows Montessori principles and seeks to understand a student's actions rather than focus on punishment. A constructivist approach centers students and keeps them connected to learning rather than excluding them from the classroom, and exclusionary practices are often connected to the school-to-prison pipeline (Fenning & Rose, 2007; Gregory et al., 2019; Helman, 2017). In the Nautilus Approach, the emphasis is placed on keeping learners in the classroom rather than removing them from the learning environment, where they lose access to the curriculum. By using constructivist approaches, public programs can more fully serve the whole child and provide greater access to a powerful classroom experience for all students, particularly BIPOC students (and even more specifically, Black students) who are most often pushed out of the classroom (Brown & Steele, 2015; Cheng, 2017).

Full Implementation: Curriculum and Standards Alignment

Increasing access connects to fully implementing Montessori in the public sector; systems that allow all children access to thrive in Montessori classrooms must be built within the wider commitment to full implementation. To support this, The Montessori Public Policy Initiative, a collaborative project of the Association Montessori International/USA (AMI/USA) and the American Montessori Society (AMS), further explained in Chapter 10, facilitated clear, shared guidelines for full implementation of Montessori in the creation of a document entitled *Montessori Essentials* (2015). These guidelines clarify for all programs to advocate for full implementation within their school district and provide communities with a rubric to measure their school's alignment.

When using these guidelines, all students will experience lessons from a trained teacher following the Montessori curriculum, with the support of other multi-age learners, in an uninterrupted work cycle. To achieve this, however, there must be alignment in curriculum and standards. Organizations and training centers are beginning to offer ways to interpret and implement Montessori curricula in calibration with national academic standards. The National **Center for Montessori in the Public Sector's (NCMPS) Montessori Curriculum to Standards Alignment (MCSA)** thoroughly aligns the Montessori lessons and the standards that provide educators with a view of how these intersect. Using **Public Montessori in Action International's (PMAI) Montessori Planning & Recordkeeping Guide (MPR)**, which holds an annual Curriculum Map for children aged 3–12, allows teachers from various Montessori training backgrounds to work from an agreed-upon sequence, aligned with the standards, offering more equitable implementation across classrooms.

By working with alignment tools in these ways, educators can provide seamless transitions for students moving through public education, offering them the full curriculum while also preparing them for a higher education experience. A South Carolina study noted that fully implemented Montessori yielded higher academic gains and better attendance and behavior (Culclasure et al., 2018). The opportunity to provide wide access to the intricate, spiraling Montessori curriculum means many more children experience school as an inspiring place to learn where they can pursue their interests motivated by intrinsic rewards rather than enforced by extrinsic motivators. There is a positive cumulative effect when students spend time in Montessori, and a 2018 study found that in later grades, Montessori students showed higher test scores (Mallett & Schroeder, 2018).

Opportunities for Full Implementation: Montessori Materials

Another opportunity for full implementation is the commitment to use the full set of Montessori materials without reliance on supplemental materials. There are weaker outcomes when Montessori classrooms dilute the learning experience with supplemental materials (Lillard & Heise, 2016). Public Montessori classrooms have the opportunity to discern which outside materials offered by the district are supplanting already existing materials (such as magnetic letters rather than the Moveable Alphabet) and which are supporting broad learning (such as teacher-made multi-step word problem practice cards). We lose full implementation of the Method when conventional materials crowd out Montessori materials in classrooms—and then, as a result, more advanced work, such as the wooden Cubing Material or advanced Sentence Analysis, is no longer used. This compromises access to the entire curriculum. Schools can remove encroaching, ever-changing conventional curriculum props and offer the full Montessori curriculum and materials for learning by streamlining classroom inventories to Montessori materials and removing other materials.

Future Directions for Public Montessori

While many challenges arise when implementing a radical pedagogy like Montessori in the public sector, there are also opportunities. Since public school districts require data collection on academic outcomes, discipline referrals, and racial disparities, public Montessorians are leaders in establishing practices to address the inequities often revealed by this level of accountability.

Taking a close look at the curriculum and instruction, developing a fair and just discipline system, engaging in thoughtful data collection and reflection, and encouraging staff exploration of systemic racism allows Montessori educators to build stronger systems that will support the growth and development of all students (Slade, 2021). Yet, these will be meaningless if they result in a watering down of the curriculum or a partial implementation of the Method. Since Montessori has a significant impact on academic and nonacademic outcomes, future directions must be towards providing greater access for all children with an uncompromised implementation (Lillard et al., 2023). The efforts toward increasing access must include an unapologetic commitment to BIPOC students and families.

If Montessori is to be implemented to its full extent, it must consider not only the physical challenges of access, but also how BIPOC students can relate to the Method. In turn, supporting Montessori educators in practicing the Method through a critical, equity-centered approach, and using the Method to inform anti-racist school practices will increase access and move public Montessori toward full implementation.

The tension that began when the Montessori Method first arrived in the United States, between maintaining the integrity of the Method and the desire to reach all children, lives on in the public sector. This tension exists alongside the opportunity to change the face of the American education system completely. We invite practitioners to acknowledge these tensions with us and reframe public Montessori's challenges as opportunities, allowing access to and the ability to fully implement the model, allowing it to serve everyone.

Additional Resources

Theoretical Models

- Critical Race Theory: *Faces at the Bottom of the Well: The Permanence of Racism* by Derrick Bell

- Critical Montessori Model: "Critical Montessori Education: Centering BIPOC Montessori Educators and their Anti-Racist Teaching Practices, Chapter 3: Theoretical Framework" by Genevieve D'Cruz https://www.proquest.com/ docview/2832692337?pq-origsite=gscholar&fromopenview=true

- Culturally Sustaining Pedagogy: *Culturally Sustaining Pedagogies: Teaching and Learning for Justice in a Changing World* by Django Paris and H. Samy Alim

- Reflecting on identity: "Examining Identity and Assimilation" from Learning for Justice https://www.learningforjustice.org/classroom-resources/lessons/ examining-identity-and-assimilation

- Introduction to Community Cultural Wealth: "Whose culture has capital? A critical race theory discussion of community cultural wealth" by Tara J. Yosso https://thrive.arizona.edu/sites/default/files/Whose%20culture%20 has%20capital_A%20critical%20race%20theory%20discussion%20 of%20community%20cultural%20wealth_1.pdf

- Supporting multilingualism in the classroom: "Recognizing community cultural wealth in classrooms" by Jennifer C. Mann https://www.ednc.org/ recognizing-community-cultural-wealth-classrooms/

- Counter-storytelling: "Welcoming Counterstory in the Primary Literacy Classroom" by Laura B. Kelly https://www.iastatedigitalpress.com/jctp/article/546/galley/426/view/

- Teaching with counter-stories: "Countering the Narrative" by Jason D. Dehart https://www.learningforjustice.org/magazine/summer-2017/countering-the-narrative

- Supporting thinking for counter-narratives: "Looking at Race and Racial Identity in Children's Books" from Learning for Justice

- https://www.learningforjustice.org/magazine/summer-2017/countering-the-narrative

- Characteristics of White Supremacy: Definitions, tools, and resources https://www.whitesupremacyculture.info/

Public School Resources

- Montessori Public Policy Initiative is an organization focused on policy and advocacy working with local groups for quality Montessori education: https://montessoriadvocacy.org/

  - Montessori Essentials: https://montessoriadvocacy.org/wp-content/uploads/2019/07/MontessoriEssentials.pdf

- National Center for Montessori in the Public Sector holds many resources to support full implementation including the Montessori Census: https://www.montessoricensus.org/ and the newspaper *Montessori Public*: https://www.montessoripublic.org/public-montessori/

  - Montessori Curriculum to Standards Alignment (MCSA)

- Public Montessori in Action International offers many trainings, collaboratives, tools, and resources to support full implementation in public schools: https://montessori-action.org/

  - The Nautilus Approach: https://montessori-action.org/nautilus

  - Montessori Planning & Recordkeeping Guide (MPR)

Discussion Questions

- How might you use the CMM to reflect on your teaching practices and pedagogy? How might you use it in your school to examine your community's systems, structures, and everyday practices?

- What steps can you take to move away from performative anti-racist work and toward action?

- What white supremacy structures are inherent in your community? In your school? In your classroom?

- How can you use a strength-based lens to examine and understand student experiences?

- What is your school doing to ensure full implementation of the Montessori Method within the public school structure?

References

Ansari, A., & Winsler, A. (2014). Montessori public school pre-k programs and the school readiness of low-income Black and Latino children. *Journal of Educational Psychology, 106*(4), 1066-1079.

Brown, K. E., & Steele, A.S.L. (2015). Racial discipline disproportionality in Montessori and traditional public schools: a comparative study using the relative rate index. *Journal of Montessori Research, 1*(1), 1–27.

Chattin-McNichols, J. (2016). The hard work of public Montessori. *Montessori Life, 28*(4), 34–45.

Cheng, D. A. (2017). Teacher racial composition and exclusion rates among Black or African American students. *Education and Urban Society, 51*(6). https://doi.org/10.1177/0013124517748724.

Culclasure, B. T., Fleming, D. J., Riga, G. (2018). *An evaluation of Montessori education in South Carolina's public schools.* The Riley Institute at Furman. https://files.eric.ed.gov/fulltext/ED622145.pdf

D'Cruz, G. (2022). Culturally sustaining practices in public Montessori schools: A landscape of the literature. *Journal of Unschooling and Alternative Learning, 16*(31), 1–20.

D'Cruz, G. (2023). Critical Montessori education: Centering BIPOC Montessori educators and their anti-racist teaching practices (30421949) [Doctoral dissertation, University of Maryland College Park].

Delgado, R., & Stefancic, J. (2017). *Critical race theory: An introduction.* New York University Press.

Debs, M. (2016). Racial and economic diversity in U.S. public Montessori schools. *Journal of Montessori Research, 2*(2), 1–34. https://doi.org/10.17161/jomr.v2i2.5848

Debs, M., & Brown, K. E. (2017). Students of color and public Montessori schools: a review of the literature. *Journal of Montessori Research, 3*(1), 1–15.

Educational Testing Service. (2019). The Montessori preschool landscape in the United States: history, programmatic inputs, availability, and effects. Debra J. Ackerman.

Fenning, P., & Rose, J. (2007). Overrepresentation of African American students in exclusionary discipline: The role of school policy. *Urban Education, 42*(6), 536–559. http://dx.doi.org/10.1177/0042085907305039

Gregory, A., Ruzek, E. A., DeCoster, J., Mikami, A. Y., & Allen, J. P. (2019). Focused classroom coaching and widespread racial equity in school discipline. *AERA open, 5*(4), 1–15. https://doi.org/10.1177/2332858419897274

Helman, D. (2017). Constructivist discipline for a student-centered classroom. *Academic Exchange Quarterly, 21*(3), 64–69.

Jones, B. L. (2020, September). *Reducing racism in schools: The promise of anti-racist policies* [Policy Brief]. University of Connecticut. Center for Policy Analysis. https://education.uconn.edu/2020/09/22/reducing-racism-in-schools-the-promise-of-anti-racist-policies/

Jor'dan, J. R. (2017). Predominantly Black institutions and public Montessori schools: reclaiming the "genius" in African American children. *Multicultural Learning and Teaching, 13*, 1–7.

Ladson-Billings, G. (1998). Just what is critical race theory and what's it doing in a *nice* field like education? *International Journal of Qualitative Studies in Education, 11*(1), 7–24. https://doi.org/10.1080/095183998236863

Leonard, A. M., & Woodland, R. H. (2022). Anti-racism is not an initiative: How professional learning communities may advance equity and social-emotional learning in schools. *Theory Into Practice, 61*(2), 212-223. https://doi.org/10.1080/00405841.2022.2036058

Lillard, A., & Heise, M. J. (2016). Removing supplementary materials from Montessori classrooms changed child outcomes. *Journal of Montessori Research, 2*(1), 16–26. https://doi.org/10.17161/jomr.v2i1.5678

Lillard, A. (2019). Shunned and admired: Montessori, self-determination, and a case for radical school reform. *Educational Psychology Review, 31*(4), 939-965. https://doi.org/10.1007/s10648-019-09483-3

Lillard, A. S., Tong, X., & Bray, P. M. (2023). Seeking racial and ethnic parity in preschool outcomes: An exploratory study of public Montessori schools vs. business-as-usual schools. *Journal of Montessori Research, 9*(1), 16–36. DOI: 10.17161/jomr.v9i1.19540.

Machado, M. (2023). Family stories matter: Critical pedagogy of storytelling in elementary classrooms. *VUE (Voices in Urban Education), 51*(1), 80–89. https://doi.org/10.35240/vue.26

Mallett, J. D., & Schroeder, J. L. (2018) Academic achievement outcomes: A comparison of Montessori and non-Montessori public elementary school students. *Journal of Elementary Education, 25*(1), 39–53.

Montessori Public Policy Initiative. (2015). *Montessori essentials.* https://montessoriadvocacy.org/wp-content/uploads/2019/07/MontessoriEssentials.pdf

Najarro, I. (2023, October). Many states are limiting how schools can teach about race. Most voters disagree. *Education Week.* https://www.edweek.org/teaching-learning/many-states-are-limiting-how-schools-can-teach-about-race-most-voters-disagree/2023/10.

Rosales, J., & Walker, T. (2021). *The racist beginnings of standardized testing.* National Education Association.

Slade, E. (2021). *Montessori in action: Building resilient Montessori schools.* Jossey-Bass.

Whitescarver, K., & Cossentino, J. (2008). Montessori and the mainstream: A century of reform on the margins. *Teachers College Record, 110*(12), 2571–2600. https://doi.org/10.1177/016146810811001

Woodland, R. H., & Mazur, R. (2018). Of teams and ties: Examining the relationship between formal and informal instructional support networks. *Educational Administration Quarterly, 55*(1), 42–72. https://doi.org/10.1177/0013161X18785

Yosso, T. J. (2005). Whose culture has capital? A critical race theory discussion of community cultural wealth. *Race Ethnicity and Education, 8*(1), 69-91. https://doi.org/10.1080/1361332052000341006

CHAPTER 5

Philosophical Underpinnings for the Incorporation of Digital Citizenship in Montessori Environments

By Dana Anderson, MS, Elizabeth Park, PhD, Seth Johnson, MS, and Zhuojing Zhang, MBA

In today's society, where technology is ubiquitous, the question inevitably arises: What would Maria Montessori, the visionary educator behind the renowned Montessori approach to education, say about the constant presence of technology in today's educational settings?

Moretti (2021) posits that the profound essence of Montessori's pedagogy was an unwavering commitment to fostering a society of peace and social justice through the empowerment of children. For Montessori, education was not merely a transmission of knowledge but a transformative journey through which children could realize their potential as architects of a better world. As we navigate the digital age, exploring Montessori's philosophy offers invaluable insights into how incorporating digital citizenship (as defined later in this chapter) aligns seamlessly with her vision for holistic child development and societal progress.

Compelling philosophical underpinnings for modern-day discussions surrounding technology and digital citizenship in Montessori environments are found in Dr. Montessori's original works. In writings and speeches, Montessori repeatedly refers to preparing children to be the masters and creators of new technologies. She eloquently stated,

Man finds himself no longer limited to his hands for the accomplishment of his desires, for he has machines. Supernature is now his desire, for he has machines. Supernature is now his background of potentiality. A wider, loftier life is his than ever before, and children have to be prepared for it, so the fundamental principle in education is correlation of all subjects and their centralization in the cosmic plan. (Montessori, 1948, p. 55)

This profound insight underscores the necessity of integrating technology into Montessori education to equip children with the skills necessary for success in the digital age. Montessori's vision extends beyond mere preparation for technological advancements. She envisioned children as the creators of a better future, asserting, "The children of today will make all the discoveries of tomorrow" (Montessori, 1946, p. 140). This underscores the imperative for educators to cultivate a generation of digital natives capable of harnessing technology for positive societal change. Furthermore, Montessori emphasized the importance of preparing children to go beyond existing knowledge and make fresh discoveries, highlighting the need for a dynamic and innovative approach to education (Montessori, 2012).

It may seem disparate to discuss technological advancements and Montessori-based peace education in the same conversation. Yet Montessori's original writings suggest an overt obligation to prepare children to be the drivers of advancements in both technology and peace (Montessori, 1946). Learning to function and communicate peacefully in our world—including the digital world—is a form of peace education. In today's terms, this is commonly known as *digital citizenship*.

After examining Montessori's writings, we believe she would assert that a framework for integrating technology—which might include exploration, experimentation, observation, and innovation—could be powerfully applied by educators, children, and adolescents across all Montessori curriculum areas. Peace education emerges as a particularly fertile ground for incorporating digital citizenship principles.

It may seem disparate to discuss technological advancements and Montessori-based peace education in the same conversation. Yet Montessori's original writings suggest an overt obligation to prepare children to be the drivers of advancements in both technology and peace (Montessori, 1946). Learning to function and communicate peacefully in our world—including the digital world—is a form of peace education. In today's terms, this is commonly known as *digital citizenship*.

Digital citizenship is also referred to as digital literacy (DQ, similar to IQ or EQ) or digital agency, and it is sometimes connected to science, technology, engineering, and math (STEM), language arts, and/or social-emotional learning (SEL) education (Manasia et al., 2018). Some common definitions of digital citizenship include concepts such as:

- Having respect, integrity, and responsibility; kindness, empathy, and tolerance; honesty, transparency, and authenticity; privacy and control of personal information (What is Cybercitizenship/Cybercitizenship.org).

- Helping children and adolescents "learn, create, and participate" in the digital world using critical thinking and "habits of mind needed to navigate digital dilemmas" while empowering them to use digital media and technology well (Common Sense Education).

- Dealing with bullying and identifying fake images and misinformation (Google's Be Internet Awesome).

- Knowing their digital rights and responsibilities; digital entrepreneurship (World Economic Forum).

- Understanding "the use, abuse, and misuse of technology" as well as the "norms of appropriate, responsible, and ethical behaviors related to online rights, roles, identity, safety, security, and communication" (NAEYC/Fred Rogers Center).

Digital citizenship has been taught in European schools for over a decade. It is now gaining solid ground as a core subject in most U.S. schools. Over 70% of U.S. schools have adopted Common Sense Education's Digital Citizenship K-12 Curriculum (Common Sense Media, n.d.). Topics such as Being Kind Online, "Red Flag Feelings," Cyberbullying, Protecting Your Digital Footprint,

Developing Healthy Relationships Online, Fair Use, and more contain lessons that fall thematically under the Montessori lessons of Grace and Courtesy, Practical Life, Language, and Peace Education, illustrating the natural integration of digital tech-based content and tools in Montessori practice. As Montessori taught shoe polishing a century ago, modern-day Practical Life lessons must include teaching children how to use tech tools and gain related digital citizenship skills. As science builds upon new discoveries, so must Montessori education build upon what we now know and have been given to empower the child.

> If education were to continue along the old lines of mere transmission of knowledge, the problem would be insoluble and there would be no hope for the world. Alone, a scientific enquiry into human personality can lead us to salvation, and we have before us in the child a psychic entity, a social group of immense size, a veritable world-power if rightly used. (Montessori, 1946, p. 1)

"Rightly used" power in the hands of multiple generations of digital natives, including the current Generation Alpha (children born between 2010–2025), requires critical knowledge acquisition of how to be good digital citizens. Just as citizens of a country need to know the rules and norms of that country to positively cohabitate with their fellow citizens and proactively contribute to their shared society, people who live large portions of their lives online (including children) need to know the rules and norms of digital society.

A special note must be made here that we Montessorians must practice digital citizenship in our own words and actions regarding our conversations about integrating technology in the Montessori environment. To build the peace we seek to teach, our discussions must include respectful dialogue about the differences of opinion in the community about this topic and how it is managed through already established community norms such as freedom within limits, mutual respect for all approaches in various environments depending on community needs and norms—high-tech, low-tech, and no-tech.

Digital citizenship lessons in the Montessori environment can integrate technology but do not *require* any use of tech. We believe all children in today's world must have the opportunity to learn this vital information about staying safe and feeling empowered as they traverse the digital landscape. And just like any other real-world tool they already use, they should also understand how technology affects their lives, positively and negatively.

Perhaps Dr. Montessori intended her cosmic curriculum to include modern technological innovations through this framework within its central principles:

> The history of human achievements is real, a living witness to the greatness of [humankind] and the children can easily be brought to thrill to the knowledge that there are millions of people like themselves, striving mentally and physically to solve the problems of life, and that all contribute to a solution though one may find it. In the field of thought as in geological eras, environment has to be prepared for an impending change. When the right preparation of thought is complete, discoveries may take place by the organization of many minds in this suitable mental atmosphere.... the fundamental principle in education is correlation of all subjects and their centralization in the cosmic plan. (Montessori, 1948, pp. 54–55)

Technology and Digital Citizenship in Montessori Classrooms

Exploring the integration of technology and digital citizenship in Montessori classrooms can lead to a robust discussion about best practices when it comes to that integration within the Montessori educational framework. These discussions can focus on appropriately maintaining Montessori's foundational principles while modernizing environments by adding new tech-oriented aspects to the curriculum. This integration represents a holistic approach to preparing children to be future leaders and innovators. If we accept Montessori's call to empower children today to use new technologies to create a better future, we can do so in ways consistent with our core values by keeping the following Montessori principles in mind.

Follow the Child and Encourage Autonomy

Establishing guidelines for developmentally appropriate use across the planes of development is central to everything we do in Montessori, and this certainly applies to the digital realm. As McNamara (2020) asserts, "How technology can aid in the child's total development is the question we must ask" (p. 225). For younger children, we can look to the joint position statement on technology of the National Association for the Education of Young Children (NAEYC) and the Fred Rogers Center for Early Learning and Children's Media at Saint Vincent College as a starting point while also examining what "concrete to abstract" and "simple to complex" mean in practice, especially for children born as digital natives who may not view those terms or experiences related to digital tech the same way non-digital native adult guides do (NAEYC, 2012). One approach could be using or building new, hands-on, concrete tools that are tangential to digital tools but do not contain a screen-based component. For example, block-based robotics kits introduce children to the basics of coding (as well as digital thinking and problem-solving skills) while also allowing them to engage in hands-on work. These and other robotic-based solutions enable screen-free options for technology integration with Montessori education (Oralbayeva et al., 2023; Zhanatkyzy et al., 2023). As students engage with digital tools and content, we must build upon Montessori's already strong foundations of empowerment within child-led environments, where intrinsic motivation as well as freedom of choice and thought are key. Additionally, it is essential that we research the impact of digital technology on developmental goals such as normalization, self-regulation, and valorization.

Prepare the Environment and Observe

Integrating digital tech-based tools in thoughtful, intentional ways informed by both broad community standards and the specific needs of individual communities is vital. Deploying a digital citizenship curriculum spanning each school year or program level can ensure students receive a comprehensive and relevant education. As students mature and move into the digital space, additional lessons can be adopted or adapted from outside organizations, or digital citizenship concepts can be integrated into existing curriculum presentations. An Acceptable

Use Policy should also be part of the prepared environment to provide clear "first period" expectations for "second period" practice around what it means to be a digital citizen. Adults must then objectively observe how students use technology and digital citizenship skills, analyze whether it serves their holistic development or acts as an obstacle, and modify environments accordingly.

Foster Cosmic and Community Connections

To build on what we do best, we can develop new components for the Montessori peace education curriculum that involve concepts related to technology and global rights, peace, and freedom. For example, work done in the Children's House related to global citizenship and conflict resolution lays the foundation, and then older students can use technology to conduct research, create presentations, and engage in coding courses, all of which expand their horizons. Moving beyond the four walls of the classroom by bringing interactive media into the prepared environment, "going out" on digital field trips, or using videoconferencing software to connect virtually with others worldwide fosters global connections. We can also engage families and strengthen local communities by providing thoughtful support and guidance to parents and caretakers on how best to prepare a home environment that fosters responsible participation in today's digital age.

Model Being a Lifelong Learner

Integrating technology in the Montessori classroom for teachers and students should be done carefully and thoughtfully, ensuring that hands-on and real-world learning remains prioritized over screen time. Educators must model on- and off-screen life balanc and become digitally literate, not only for the students in their care, but also to leverage technology's convenience for their own benefit, such as reducing

Integrating a digital citizenship curriculum in all Montessori environments is both philosophically sound and essential for equipping children with the skills and knowledge needed to succeed in a rapidly evolving world. By embracing technology intentionally, Montessori educators can empower students to become responsible digital citizens and leaders in the current century.

teacher workload and innovating lessons and materials. For example, administrators and guides may choose to use tech-based tools to track student progress or as a tool for observation.

Integrating a digital citizenship curriculum in all Montessori environments is both philosophically sound and essential for equipping children with the skills and knowledge needed to succeed in a rapidly evolving world. By embracing technology intentionally, Montessori educators can empower students to become responsible digital citizens and leaders in the current century.

Digital Citizenship and Diversity, Equity, Inclusion

Montessori's vision of education as a transformative force, and especially the concept "if rightly used" (Montessori, 1946, p. 1), begs the exploration of the integration of diversity, equity, and inclusion (DEI) principles within technology in Montessori education.

Ensuring all students have equal opportunities to utilize technological resources aligns with the essence of individualized learning central to Montessori pedagogy (Means, 2010). This prioritization of equitable access is essential for creating an inclusive educational environment where every child's unique needs are met. Moreover, culturally responsive educational technology plays a vital role in this pursuit, as it reflects and respects the diverse cultural backgrounds of Montessori students (Eppard et al., 2021; Luiken, 2020). By selecting and designing digital tools that resonate with learners' cultural identities, educators uphold the principles of DEI while supporting personalized learning experiences.

Inclusive app design, tailored to accommodate diverse learning needs, further echoes Montessori's philosophy of catering to individual learning styles and abilities (Alehegn & Keller, 2019; Rose & Meyer, 2002). Emphasizing cultural sensitivity in digital resources enhances their efficacy, particularly for English language learners in Montessori classrooms (Orosco & O'Connor, 2014). Engaging families/caregivers and broader school communities in discussions surrounding technology integration fosters a collaborative approach rooted in shared values. This inclusive ethos extends to professional development initiatives aimed at equipping educators with the necessary skills to seamlessly integrate technology in alignment with DEI principles (Nansen et al., 2014). Ongoing training ensures educators can adapt to the evolving landscape of inclusive design practices, enhancing their ability to meet the diverse needs of Montessori learners.

In essence, the fusion of DEI principles with educational technology in Montessori classrooms represents a holistic approach to fostering inclusivity and individual growth. By embracing diversity, prioritizing equity, and nurturing a culture of inclusion (regarding technology and beyond), Montessori education realizes its capacity as a transformative force, empowering every child to thrive in an ever-changing world (Park & Murray, 2022). This aligns with Dr. Montessori's vision of education as a means to unlock the potential of every child, thereby contributing to societal progress (Montessori, 1946).

In digital citizenship, it is imperative to consider diverse perspectives and voices to ensure inclusivity and equity in access and representation. Organizations like the World Economic Forum, the Digital Youth Network, AI for Equity, and the Algorithmic Justice League offer valuable insights into global trends and challenges related to digital access, bias, and citizenship, providing a platform for dialogue and collaboration on DEI initiatives. As educators, we must continuously examine and be lifelong learners, adapting our practices to meet the evolving needs of our students and communities.

Conclusion

Dr. Montessori strongly asserted that we are not to conform to or teach the status quo, but rather to be keen observers and forward thinkers who assist children in their task of becoming the makers of a new society—a society that would include new problems and opportunities, questions and wonders that were far beyond the reach of the adult imagination of her time—precisely what many of today's technological advances embody.

Leaders in technology, ethics, education, law, philosophy, and geopolitics are sounding a clarion call. The World Economic Forum stresses the immediate need for young people to be prepared for the technological, social, economic, and geopolitical sea changes that will continue to happen as the rate of technological advancements continues ever more rapidly. Duke University law professor and philosopher Dr. Nita Farahany is leading the call at the global community level to enshrine cognitive liberty and freedom of thought as a Universal Human Right by the United Nations (Anderson, 2023).

Dr. Montessori's poignant observation highlights the urgency of the challenges facing modern society:

> Society has not only developed into a state of utmost complication and extreme contrasts, but it has now come to a crisis in which the peace of the world and civilization itself are threatened. The crisis is certainly connected with the immense progress that has been made in science and its practical applications, but it has not been caused by them. More than to anything else it is due to the fact that the development of man himself has not kept pace with that of his external environment. (Montessori, 2007, p. 71)

Dr. Montessori strongly asserted that we are not to conform to or teach the status quo, but rather to be keen observers and forward thinkers who assist children in their task of becoming the makers of a new society—a society that would include new problems and opportunities, questions and wonders that were far beyond the reach of the adult imagination of her time —precisely what many of today's technological advances embody.

As Dr. Montessori contends, this crisis stems not solely from technological advancements but from humanity's failure to evolve at a comparable pace. As we navigate these challenges, Montessori educational philosophy and sound digital citizenship practices present us with a beacon of hope to meet a new need in the holistic development of individuals. In this era of rapid technological change, we must empower children, adolescents, and educators to grow within the complex challenges of our time. With Dr. Montessori's words as our guide, we can confidently empower young people by helping them learn digital citizenship concepts and skills, knowing they are the creators of a society of peace and advancements yet unknown.

Discussion Questions

- How might you incorporate digital citizenship into your environment?

- What are your personal feelings about integrating technology into the Montessori curriculum?

- Do you have an Acceptable Use Policy for digital tech tools and AI-created content at your school? If not, how can your community begin to develop one?

- Most children in our care are "digital natives," understanding and working with technology in a way we adults may never grasp. What opportunities are there for you to learn from your students when it comes to technology?

- What digital tools and strategies can be used to embrace diversity, ensure equity, and foster a culture of inclusion in Montessori classrooms?

References

Alehegn, T., & Keller, R. (2019). Mobile apps, universal design, and accessibility in schools: Creating an inclusive classroom experience. In D. Mentor (Ed.), *Advancing mobile learning in contemporary educational spaces* (pp. 317–343). IGI Global.

Anderson, D. (2023, November 1). *Montessori education in the age of neurotechnology: A conversation with labposium keynote speaker Dr. Nita Farahany [Online blog post]*. American Montessori Society. https://amshq.org/Blog/2023-11-01-Montessori-Education-in-the-Age-of-Neurotechnology

Common Sense Media. (n.d.). Everything you need to teach digital citizenship. Common Sense Education. Retrieved April 1, 2023 from https://www.commonsense.org/education/digital-citizenship

Eppard, J., Kaviani, A., Bowles, M., & Johnson, J. (2021). EdTech culturation: Integrating a culturally relevant pedagogy into educational technology. *The Electronic Journal of e-Learning, 19*(6), pp. 516–530.

Luiken, D. D. (2020). Culturally responsive teaching within a Montessori learning environment [Master's capstone] Hamline University, Saint Paul, Minnesota. Retrieved from https://digitalcommons.hamline.edu/hse_cp/497?utm_source=digitalcommons.hamline.edu%2Fhse_cp%2F497&utm_medium=PDF&utm_campaign=PDFCoverPages

Manasia, L., Negreanu, M.-C., & Macovei, M. (2018). *Is Q for DQ? Applying Q-methodology for researching digital intelligence.* Proceedings of The International Scientific Conference eLearning and Software for Education, Romania, 3, 84-89.

McNamara, J. (2020). Technology and its use in a Montessori environment. *The NAMTA Journal 44*(1), 224–232.

Means, B. (2010). Technology and education change: Focus on student learning. *Journal of Research on Technology in Education, 42*(3), 285–307.

Montessori, M. (1946). *Education for a new world.* Kalakshetra Publications.

Montessori, M. (1948). *To educate the human potential.* Kalakshetra Publications.

Montessori, M. (2007). *From childhood to adolescence (The Montessori Series Vol. 12).* Montessori-Pierson Publishing Company.

Montessori, M. (2012). *The 1946 London lectures (The Montessori Series Vol. 17).* Montessori-Pierson Publishing Company.

Moretti, E. (2021). *The best weapon for peace: Maria Montessori, education, and children's rights.* The University of Wisconsin Press.

Nansen, B., Wilken, R., Arnold, M., & Gibbs, M. (2014). Digital literacies and the national broadband network: Competency, legibility, context. *Media International Australia, 145*(1). 64–74.

National Association for the Education of Young Children (NAEYC) & Fred Rogers Center for Early Learning and Children's Media at Saint Vincent College. (2012). *Technology and interactive media as tools in early childhood programs serving children from birth through age 8* [Position statement]. NAEYC.

Orosco, M. J., & O'Connor, R. (2014). Culturally responsive instruction for English language learners with learning disabilities. *Journal of Learning Disabilities, 47*(6), 515–531.

Park, E., & Murray, A. (2022). Montessori education in the digital age. In A. Murray, M. Debs, M. McKenna, & E-M. T. Ahlquist (Eds.), *The Bloomsbury handbook of Montessori education* (pp. 763–779). Bloomsbury Publishing.

Rose, D. H., & Meyer, A. (2002). *Teaching every student in the digital age: Universal design for Learning.* ASCD.

CHAPTER 6

From Seed to Society: Sustainability Education in Montessori Contexts

By Sinead Meehan, PhD, and Geoffrey Bishop

We cannot protect something we do not love, we cannot love what we do not know, and we cannot know what we do not see. Or hear. Or sense.

(Louv, 2012, p. 104)

Our Earth and its multispecies are in crisis. From poverty, food insecurity, gender inequality, and the lack of access to clean drinking water to rising greenhouse gas emissions, plastic pollution, deforestation, and the acidification of our oceans, there is a clear need for collective action (Guterres, 2023; United Nations, 2023). Reflecting on the sustainability issues of today, we must pause and ask ourselves, how did we get here, and what can we do, through our Montessori pedagogy, to collectively construct a better tomorrow?

This chapter explores the concepts of sustainability and sustainable development, examines education for sustainable development both broadly and in Montessori contexts, and discusses actionable steps Montessori guides can take to support the development of children and adults who support ecological, human, and economic health and vitality over time (Regents of the University of California, 2023).

Sustainability and Sustainable Development

The word *sustainability* is derived from the Latin word *sustinere*, which means to *maintain, support, uphold,* or *endure* (Harper, 2023b). Similar to its Latin origins, *sustainable development* is defined by the United Nations as "development that meets the needs of the present without compromising the ability of future generations to meet their own needs" (Brundtland, 1987, p. 41). This definition recognizes that humans will engage in activities that impact each other and the environment and must consciously act in ways that allow social, economic, and environmental flourishing to endure over time.

Sustainability and sustainable development conceptualizations differ based on the worldviews, values, and historical contexts of cultural groups. For example, Western conceptualizations, which we define as conceptualizations stemming from Europe and those countries settled by Europeans, especially the United States, Canada, Australia, and New Zealand, often reflect an anthropocentric perspective, treating nature as a set of resources to be managed. Within this framing, there is a strong emphasis on individual actions and responsibilities, focusing on scientific knowledge and technological solutions. The Western approach is highly influenced by capitalistic endeavors and political cycles, focusing on economic growth, globalization, and short-term outcomes, reflecting a linear understanding of time.

In contrast, Indigenous conceptualizations of sustainability are often rooted in a holistic worldview. We define Indigenous conceptualizations as those stemming from any group of people who lived in a specific region "before colonists or settlers arrived, defined new borders, and began to occupy the land" (Healthline, 2021, para. 3). Indigenous perspectives view humans as interconnected with nature, emphasizing reciprocity and respect for all living beings. Long-term sustainability is prioritized, as evidenced by doctrines such as the Seventh Generation Principle, which instructs individuals to consider the impact of their decisions on the next seven generations (Indigenous Corporate Training, Inc., 2020). Furthermore, Indigenous perspectives view sustainability as a collective responsibility; therefore, community involvement and intergenerational knowledge are crucial in shaping, sharing, and implementing sustainability practices. In Indigenous communities, Traditional Ecological Knowledge (TEK), which integrates spiritual, cultural, and practical understandings of the environment, is passed down, often orally, from generation to generation (Charles & Cajete, 2020). Indigenous perspectives focus less on economic growth and more on utilizing local resources for sustenance.

While comparing these two broad perspectives does not account for the nuanced views of each cultural group or the individuals that compose them, it highlights major differences between the two approaches. It forces us to consider the criticality of drawing upon multiple knowledge systems or ways of knowing when designing and implementing comprehensive and effective sustainability efforts (Mazzocchi, 2020). Socially-just sustainability efforts must advocate for and adopt a pluralistic, multilevel perspective. While a multitude of Indigenous and local ways of knowing exist and are at times acknowledged, reductionist and anthropocentric views of sustainability continue to dominate our global views on sustainability. Martin and colleagues (2020) remind us that "these failures to recognize knowledge diversity become institutionalized in education systems, government, and even environmental organizations, ignoring deep cultural values and constraining policy learning" (p. 27).

Furthermore, from a multilevel perspective, governments, legislatures, the private sector, and civil society must work in partnership to address sustainability issues. Historically, the impetus for change has been placed on the individual; however, using the storyline of David and Goliath, Geels (2014) argues that we must "shift the analytical agenda to better understand how 'Goliath' [governments, corporations, etc.] can be weakened, eroded and destabilized, to enhance the chances of green Davids [innovations]" (p. 37).

Education for Sustainable Development

In response to a global push for sustainable development, the United Nations Educational, Scientific and Cultural Organization (UNESCO) (n.d.) developed a global framework called *education for sustainable development* (ESD), which "aims to bring about the personal and societal transformation that is necessary to change course from challenges such as climate change, loss of biodiversity, unsustainable use of resources, and inequality," by "addressing environmental, social, and economic issues in a holistic way" using educative means (para. 1). Education for sustainable development was born out of UNESCO's call to address salient global challenges, including climate change, loss of biodiversity, unsustainable use of resources, and inequality. Operationally speaking, UNESCO has advocated for accomplishing the ESD program by integrating the 2030 Agenda's 17 Sustainable Development Goals (SDGs) into learning through "action-oriented, transformative pedagog[ies], which supports self-directed learning, participation and collaboration, problem-orientation, inter – and transdisciplinarity and the linking of formal and informal learning" (UNESCO, 2017, p. 7).

Education for sustainable development, however, requires a fine balance of increasing students' awareness of the acuteness and severity of sustainability issues and their underlying causes while maintaining a sense of hope for the future and the ability to affect positive change (Vandaele & Stålhammar, 2022). Today's students show increasing concern and anxiety around the impact of anthropogenic actions and the lack of tangible solutions that can be readily implemented at the individual level (IPCC, 2018; Pihkala, 2020). Therefore, students' awareness of these negative emotions (Smith and Leiserowitz, 2014; Stevenson et al., 2014; Yang and Kahlor, 2013) must be paired with a sense of hope, as hope is linked to proactive and long-term engagement (Li and Monroe, 2019; Vandaele & Stålhammar, 2022). In the context of ESD, hope emerges as a crucial coping mechanism against despair, igniting the belief that the future remains malleable, thereby empowering individuals with the notion that they can collectively shape the destiny of the planet and the multispecies that occupy it (Debaise & Stengers, 2016).

In addition, Vandaele and Stålhammar (2022) argue that "the implementation of ESD requires paying attention to each student's individual processes, including the different stages of knowledge acquisition, critical analysis, personal and collective commitment, proactivity and how cognitive and socioemotional learning develops certain tipping points for transformative action" (p. 274). In other words, ESD requires us to *follow the child* (Montessori, 1992, 1995). In order to *follow the child*, Montessori (1992, 1995) argued that guides must be keen observers, understanding and attending to each child's unique interests, needs, and developmental stages. In doing so, guides create an environment that can empower children to make choices about their education, promoting a sense of ownership and engagement in the learning process.

Montessori and Sustainability

Montessori embraced sustainability in all areas. Through her approach to education, Montessori (1950) articulated that:

> The child [would] develop a kind of philosophy which teaches this unity of the universe; this is the very thing to motivate his interest and to give him a better insight into his own place and task in the world and at the same time presenting a chance for the development of his creative energy. (as cited in Stephenson, 2013, pp. 119-120)

Through cosmic education, Montessori believed we could restore harmony and order to the world, enabling humanity to realize its true potential. She envisioned a sustainable education system that protected the dignity and education of every child. She identified nature and empathy as essential components of every child's education, from immersion in the outdoors to observing and caring for plants and animals through all phases of life to tending gardens and farms. Montessori adopted a systems thinking approach (Montessori, 2015), ensuring that children made sense of the complexities of the world by looking at concepts in terms of wholes and relationships rather than individualistic parts. For example, the lesson "Where does our bread come from?" fosters an understanding of production and consumption patterns, including the importance of individuals' roles in the free market. These ideas are not just words on paper but the underpinning and glue that holds the Montessori philosophy and pedagogy together.

> Through cosmic education, Montessori believed we could restore harmony and order to the world, enabling humanity to realize its true potential. She envisioned a sustainable education system that protected the dignity and education of every child.

Embracing Montessori's vision for education, Montessori schools have actively addressed sustainability issues through two primary methods: (1) The Montessori curriculum and (2) initiatives born out of students' interests or a school's unique needs. Montessori schools adhering to the Montessori curriculum present lessons that address issues related to sustainable development on a daily basis. For instance, Elementary students may engage in Practical Life lessons on conserving energy by turning off lights and electronics that are not in use, or by line drying classroom laundry.

In other instances, student-led endeavors initiate sustainability efforts. For example, Lewis and Baudains (2007) describe an instance where 2 Montessori students decided they wanted to power their school using solar energy. The two students prepared a detailed report and presented it to the school's Management Committee. Once approved, the students started fundraising, learning about solar panels, and promoting solar power. They obtained community support through partnerships with various businesses, organizations, and government departments. The student-led initiative eventually became an endeavor for the whole school. Pre-Primary students washed and cleaned the second-hand solar panels, while the Upper Primary students tested them to ensure they were in working order. The students used publicity through radio appearances, store displays, and articles to promote solar energy and support their fundraising efforts. Four years after the idea's inception, the school officially flipped the switch to turn on the school's solar power system.

Although the Montessori philosophy guides our development as citizens of the world, we must also take a systems thinking approach, understanding children's development within the context of today's society and the world they will grow into. While post-industrialization and the dramatic reinvention of society have propelled us through two centuries of rapid growth, we have, in many instances, lost sight of the true purpose of education. Our planet and civil society are under threat, and our idea of preparing students for the future is still rooted in an industrialized societal mentality. According to Stevenson (2007), there exists a "discrepancy between the problem-solving and action-oriented goals associated with the contemporary philosophy of environmental education and an emphasis on the acquisition of environmental knowledge and awareness in school programs" (p. 139). We argue that future generations need skills in systemic, strategic, critical, and creative thinking in order to identify and address problems and their root causes at local, national, and global levels.

Although the Montessori philosophy guides our development as citizens of the world, we must also take a systems thinking approach, understanding children's development within the context of today's society and the world they will grow into. While post-industrialization and the dramatic reinvention of society have propelled us through two centuries of rapid growth, we have, in many instances, lost sight of the true purpose of education.

Actionable Steps for Montessori Guides

To bring Montessori's vision of sustainability education to life, guides should think creatively, making explicit connections between their lessons and sustainable development goals. To demonstrate this in practice, we present multiple examples of Education for Sustainable Development implemented in Montessori classrooms and describe how each is linked to the 2030 Sustainable Development Agenda and the 17 Sustainable Development Goals (United Nations, 2015).

Sustainable Development Goal 12:
Responsible Production and Consumption
("Ensure sustainable consumption and production patterns")

At Nature's Classroom Institute (NCI, in Mukwonago, WI), a non-profit focused on the connection between the natural environment and future generations, guides introduce the concept of making good choices through the topic of food waste. Approximately 30–40% of the food supply in the United States is believed to be wasted (USDA, 2023). At NCI, the term *ort* conveys the importance and power of "making good choices about food." *Ort,* which comes from Old English, means "remains of food left from a meal, table scrap" (Harper, 2023b). At NCI, this simple word has made a huge impact. *Ort* is grounded in the philosophy of thinking first, acting second. It reminds members of the NCI community that they have the ability to choose and that their choices have an impact on our planet's sustainability. *Ort* encourages community members to serve appropriate portions, try foods before taking them, and take personal accountability to reduce waste.

As described here, *ort* is about making good food choices and is closely linked to *SDG 12: Responsible Production and Consumption.* Since embracing *ort* as a value at NCI nearly 30 years ago, the organization has observed significant changes in the community's food waste practices, including reducing food waste from 13–15 pounds per day to under 2 pounds per day. The success of *ort* at NCI is in alignment with other studies which suggest that emphasizing social norms and motivational goals, along with "nudging" (Thaler & Sunstein, 2009), can have a positive impact on individuals' choices (Abrahamse, 2020; Monroe et al., 2015; Sparkman & Walton, 2017). Other examples of *ort* in action could include creating a communal snack cart where students place food they do not plan on eating rather than disposing of them or teaching students responsible for planning the snack menu to strategically plan their grocery list to reduce potential food waste.

Moving beyond the practical application of *ort*, Montessori guides may want to engage students in lessons on how food loss occurs at every stage, from production to distribution to consumption. For example, guides might pose questions such as: (a) How might extreme weather or natural disasters such as flooding or drought impact a farmer's crops?; (b) How might exposure to insects, rodents, birds, molds, and bacteria affect food products?; or (c) What might happen if equipment malfunctions in transport or at the retailer (i.e., the refrigeration component breaks)? In addition, guides can address additional approaches for dealing with food waste. Aside from responsible consumption, leftover food may be donated to hunger-relief organizations (SDG 2: Zero Hunger), composted or recycled into other products such as animal feed (SDG 12: Responsible Production and Consumption, SDG 13: Climate Action, and SDG 15: Life on Land), or turned into a source of bioenergy (SDG 7: Affordable and Clean Energy).

Sustainable Development Goal 17: Partnerships for the Goals ("Strengthen the means of implementation and revitalize the Global Partnership for Sustainable Development")

Many Montessori schools have developed meaningful partnerships with local, national, and international organizations in an effort to support sustainable development efforts, meeting SDG 17: Partnerships for the Goals. As Ashley Causey-Golden, the creator of Afrocentric Montessori and co-founder of Gather Forest School reminds us, "Books can only do so much. Montessori guides need to bring community into their classrooms" (personal communication, June 6, 2024). While the goals each partnership works towards may vary, the overall aim of SDG 17 is for different sectors and actors to work together in an integrated manner, sharing their financial resources, knowledge, and expertise.

To provide a local example, the Gather Forest School partnered with Joyful Jarra, a refillery and sustainable goods store. According to Joyful Jarra (2024), "refilleries exist to address the huge waste problem caused by plastic and packaging [by selling goods that] are eco-friendly, sustainable, and package-free" (para. 2).

Through this partnership, students at Gather Forest School were able to connect the practical life activities they engage in daily (i.e. brushing teeth, washing hands, doing laundry) with the products used to complete those tasks (i.e. toothpaste, toothbrushes, soap, and laundry detergent), recognizing their impact and brainstorming feasible ways to be more sustainable stewards of the planet (A. Causey-Golden, personal communication, June 6, 2024).

At the regional and state level, Williamsburg Montessori School (WMS, in Williamsburg, VA) has an ongoing partnership with the Chesapeake Bay Foundation and Oyster Reef Keepers of Virginia to tackle SDG 14: Life Below Water. The Chesapeake Bay Foundation seeks to "fight for effective, science-based solutions to the pollution degrading the Chesapeake Bay" (CBF, 2024a), while the Oyster Reef Keepers of Virginia "aim to re-establish [the oyster] species in waterways throughout coastal Virginia" (CBF, 2024b) through efforts such as oyster gardening, reef ball production, shell bagging, and recycling.

As part of their aquaculture and bay studies work, WMS students act as stewards of the environment by growing oysters to be placed on protective reefs. In this way, they embody the principles of Erdkinder but are branded *Wasserkinder* ("children of the water") to match their commitment and activities to serve and sustain the largest estuary in the nation and the most productive watershed in the world. While oyster restoration in the Chesapeake Bay is making significant strides, colonization, overharvesting, and commercialization over the centuries have devastated the oyster reefs, which once "lay as thick as stones" (UMCES, 2024).

In addition to oyster gardening, WMS students also promote the overall health of the Bay through community engagement and public education, pulling Practical Life and citizen science into their interdisciplinary curriculum. For instance, the Chesapeake Bay National Estuarine Research Reserve-VA(CBNERR) hosts a fun, family-friendly Discovery Lab series once a month. According to the Virginia Institute of Marine Science (2024b), "each lab focuses on a specific topic through a series of stations that provide hands-on activities for kids and adults" (para. 9) with the overall aim of increasing the public's knowledge and understanding of their local environment and the issues it faces and influencing their behaviors and attitudes in an effort to restore and conserve the bay. WMS Middle School students have hosted a Discovery Lab at the Chesapeake Bay National Estuarine Research Reserve-VA on the topics "Fish of the Bay," and "The Spiny World of Echinoderms." Alongside the work being conducted through the Middle School's aquaculture and bay studies program, WMS encourages students and families at all levels to engage in watershed stewardship and maintenance through community events such as Clean the Bay Day (CBF, 2024c) at York River State Park and "Catch the King" Tide (VIMS, 2024a) each fall semester in what is lauded as the world's largest environmental survey.

Partnerships that build students' environmental literacy are not reserved for suburban and rural areas. Ashley Causey-Golden points out that "if we label nature as being in a forest or on a lake, we are cutting out huge groups of people" and asks us to consider how land has been distributed over time (personal communication, June 6, 2024). For instance, when the Lenape inhabited the island of Mannahatta in the early seventeenth century, there were approximately 220,000 acres of oyster beds in the harbor. However, colonization and its effects, such as over-harvesting, water pollution, and industrialization, wiped out the New York City Harbor's oyster population. Recognizing the important role of oysters in cleaning the harbor of pollutants, providing shelter for other wildlife, mitigating the impact of powerful waves, minimizing the risk of flooding, and preventing shoreline erosion, the Billion Oyster Project works in collaboration with New York City communities to restore the oyster reefs in New York Harbor. The project views education and connection with the natural world as essential to changing human behavior and is committed to placing students at the forefront of the initiative to revive oyster reefs in New York Harbor, reaching 100 schools and 11,000 students in New York City (Billion Oyster Project, 2024).

Sustainable Development Goal 15: Life on Land ("Protect, restore and promote sustainable use of terrestrial ecosystems, sustainably manage forests, combat desertification, and halt and reverse land degradation and halt biodiversity loss")

Outdoor education is another means of developing students' environmental awareness and sustainability practices. While definitions of outdoor education vary widely, most consider outdoor education to be any form of organized learning that occurs outdoors. Western, twentieth-century outdoor education models are largely separate from the aims of education for sustainable development and instead focus on adventure activities and principles for personal growth and development (Hill, 2012). For example, students may go on a day-long canoe trip or a week-long camping trip to develop a range of skills, from navigating unfamiliar territory and cooking meals over a self-built fire to team-work and flexibility. Conversely, there are many organizations advocating for "more meaningful and critical engagement with human/nature relationships, place, culture, and ecology" (Hill, 2012, p. 15). Much like Dr. Montessori, these organizations see the outdoor environment as a natural extension of the classroom.

At Keres Children's Learning Center (KCLC, in Cochiti Pueblo, NM), outdoor education is a means of recentering land-based child-rearing practices that have been around for centuries but are in direct opposition to the settler colonial norms of individualism, economic growth, and passivity. KCLC engages its learners in outdoor education through intergenerational nature walks to counteract these hegemonic norms. Moquino and colleagues (2023) explain that:

> This intergenerational approach restores the ancient methods of teaching young children essential life skills and foster[s] community and land fluency that leads to strong Indigenous language exposure in naturalistic settings and opportunities for developing academic foundation through various learning settings like the outdoors. (p. 128)

Nature walks at KCLC allow children to build relationships with elders and allow elders to share intergenerational skills and knowledge, Cochiti values, and the Keres language. Elders are recognized by community members based on their wisdom, knowledge, and skills, as opposed to their age (Wilson, 2003). Nature walks allow children to have direct contact with their natural environment and provide opportunities for spontaneous learning. They may learn the name of a new plant in Keres and English or be taught the value of the plant life with whom they are in relation. In addition to sharing knowledge, skills, values, and language with children, nature walks promote movement, an often-overlooked aspect of development in traditional K–12 settings, and which can cultivate a range of executive function skills (Moquino et al., 2023).

Indigenous perspectives on sustainability align with research on the importance of people's connection to nature. Exposing children to nature, whether it be through outdoor education or unstructured outdoor play, has numerous benefits, including a positive impact on children's mental health (McCormick, 2017), play and motor development (Fjørtoft, 2004), academic performance (Schutte et al., 2017), and social development (Barton et al., 2015; McCurdy et al., 2010; Mutz & Müller, 2016).

Conclusion

In conclusion, exploring education for sustainable development within Montessori contexts prompts us to reflect deeply on our responsibility to understand and teach about sustainability challenges and their root causes. Concurrently, it urges us to cultivate hope and foster the growth of justice-oriented stewards of our planet. As expressed by Greses Perez (2024), "If realities can be constructed, they can be changed." Transformative change demands acknowledging the disparities in sustainability outcomes arising from power imbalances and implementing efforts to challenge and diminish these entrenched systems and their influence (Martin et al., 2020).

At the heart of this call to action is the belief that implementing the Montessori philosophy has the potential to nurture individuals who understand the principles of sustainability and actively embody them in their daily lives. Montessori pedagogy can contribute significantly to the collective effort toward global sustainability through a commitment to fostering love, care, and a deep-seated connection to the world. As we look ahead, it is clear that the impact of Montessori education extends far beyond the classroom, shaping generations of individuals who embrace the responsibility to safeguard the well-being of our planet and its diverse inhabitants.

Acknowledgments

The authors would like to acknowledge Ashley Causey-Golden, the creator of Afrocentric Montessori and co-founder of Gather Forest School, Corinna Ferro, Middle School Director and Secondary Educator at Williamsburg Montessori School, and Dale Naranjo, Outdoor Educator at Keres Children's Learning Center for their insights and contributions to this chapter.

Discussion Questions

- What are some ways that you empower students to collectively shape the destiny of the planet?

- How will you instill a sense of hope, linked to proactive and long-term engagement in sustainability efforts?

- How do you nurture students to understand sustainability principles and actively embody them daily?

References

Abrahamse, W. (2020). How to effectively encourage sustainable food choices: a mini-review of available evidence. *Frontiers in Psychology, 11*, 589674. https://10.3389/fpsyg.2020.589674

Barton, J., Sandercock, G., Pretty, J., & Wood, C. (2015). The effect of playground-and nature-based playtime interventions on physical activity and self-esteem in UK school children. *International Journal of Environmental Health Research, 25*(2), 196–206. https://doi.org/10.1080/09603123.2014.915020

Billion Oyster Project. (2024). *Education.* Billion Oyster Project. https://www.billion-oysterproject.org/stem-education

Brundtland, G. (1987). Report of the World commission on environment and development: Our common future. United Nations General Assembly document A/42/427.

Charles, C., & Cajete, G. A. (2020). Wisdom traditions, science and care for the earth: Pathways to responsible action. *Ecopsychology, 12*(2), 65–70. https://doi.org/10.1089/eco.2020.0020

Chesapeake Bay Foundation (CBF). (2024a). Our mission. About the Chesapeake Bay Foundation. https://www.cbf.org/about-cbf/our-mission/?gad_source=1&gclid=C-j0KCQiAhc-sBhCEARIsAOVwHuSwoa8zHOYFpfaBd_63v6ZmsoHU8g1zDJIg-jWa0GnNTCw7rcSGtd94aAh7ZEALw_wcB

Chesapeake Bay Foundation (CBF). (2024b). How we save the Bay. Programs and initiatives. https://www.cbf.org/how-we-save-the-bay/programs-initiatives/virginia/oyster-restoration/index.html#:~:text=The%20program%20includes%20producing%20baby,be%20used%20on%20future%20reefs.

Chesapeake Bay Foundation (CBF). (2024c). Clean the Bay day. Events. https://www.cbf.org/events/clean-the-bay-day/

Debaise, D. and Stengers, I. (2016). The insistence of the possible: Towards a speculative pragmatism. *Multitudes, 65*(4), 82-89. https://doi.org/10.3917/mult.065.0082

Fjørtoft, I. (2004). Landscape as playscape: The effects of natural environments on children's play and motor development. *Children Youth and Environments, 14*(2), 21–44.

Geels, F. W. (2014). Regime resistance against low-carbon transitions: Introducing politics and power into the multi-level perspective. *Theory, Culture & Society, 31*(5), 21–40. https://doi.org/10.1177/0263276414531627

Guterres, A. (2023, July 27). Press conference by Secretary-General António Guterres at United Nations Headquarters. United Nations Meeting Coverage and Press Releases. https://press.un.org/en/2023/sgsm21893.doc.htm

Harper, D. (2023a). Ort. https://www.etymonline.com/word/ort

Harper, D. (2023b). Sustainable. https://www.etymonline.com/word/sustainable

Healthline. (2021, March). What does 'Indigenous' mean? How to use it (and when to avoid it). https://www.healthline.com/health/what-does-indigenous-mean#:~:-text=%E2%80%9CIndigenous%E2%80%9D%20describes%20any%20group%20of,began%20to%20occupy%20the%20land.

Hill, A. (2012). Developing approaches to outdoor education that promote sustainability education. *Journal of Outdoor and Environmental Education, 16,* 15–27. https://doi.org/10.1007/BF03400935

Indigenous Corporate Training, Inc. (2020, May 30). What is the seventh generation principle? https://www.ictinc.ca/blog/seventh-generation-principle#:~:text=May%2030%2C%202020,seven%20generations%20into%20the%20future.

Intergovernmental Panel on Climate Change (IPCC). (2018). Global Warming of 1.5°C. An IPCC Special Report on the impacts of global warming of 1.5°C above pre-industrial levels and related global greenhouse gas emission pathways, in the context of strengthening the global response to the threat of climate change, sustainable development, and efforts to eradicate poverty. Cambridge University Press. https://doi.org/10.1017/9781009157940.001.

Joyful Jarra. (2024). *About us.* Joyful Jarra. https://joyfuljarra.com/pages/about-us

Lewis, E., & Baudains, C. (2007). Whole systems thinking: Education for sustainability at a Montessori school. *Eingana, 301*(1), 9–11.

Li, C. J., & Monroe, M. C. (2019). Exploring the essential psychological factors in fostering hope concerning climate change. *Environmental Education Research, 25*(6), 936–954. https://doi.org/10.1080/13504622.2017.1367916

Louv, R. (2012). *The nature principle: Reconnecting with life in a virtual Age.* Algonquin Books.

Martin, A., Armijos, M. T., Coolsaet, B., Dawson, N., AS Edwards, G., Few, R., Gross-Camp, N., Rodriguez, I., Schroeder, H, Tebboth, M.G.L., & White, C. S. (2020). Environmental justice and transformations to sustainability. *Environment: Science and Policy for Sustainable Development, 62*(6), 19–30. https://doi.org/10.1080/00139157.2020.1820294

Mazzocchi, F. (2020). A deeper meaning of sustainability: Insights from indigenous knowledge. *The Anthropocene Review, 7*(1), 77-93. https://doi.org/10.1177/2053019619898888

McCormick, R. (2017). Does access to green space impact the mental well-being of children: A systematic review. *Journal of Pediatric Nursing, 37,* 3–7. https://doi.org/10.1016/j.pedn.2017.08.027

McCurdy, L. E., Winterbottom, K. E., Mehta, S. S., & Roberts, J. R. (2010). Using nature and outdoor activity to improve children's health. *Current Problems in Pediatric and Adolescent Health Care, 40*(5), 102–117. https://doi.org/10.1016/j. cppeds.2010.02.003

Monroe, J. T., Lofgren, I. E., Sartini, B. L., & Greene, G. W. (2015). The Green Eating Project: web-based intervention to promote environmentally conscious eating behaviours in US university students. *Public Health Nutrition, 18*(13), 2368–2378. https://doi.org/10.1017/s1368980015002396

Montessori, M. (1950). *University of Amsterdam lecture.*

Montessori, M. (1992). *From childhood to adolescents.* ABC-Clio.

Montessori, M. (1995). *The absorbent mind.* Holt Paperbacks.

Montessori, M. (2015). *To educate the human potential.* Ravenio Books.

Moquino, T. L., Allison-Burbank, J.D., Blum-Martinez, R., & Kitchens, K. (2023). Walk with us: Indigenous approaches to developmentally appropriate practice. In I. Alanís & T. Sturdivant (Eds) *Focus on developmentally appropriate practice: Equitable & joyful learning in preschool.* NAEYC.

Mutz, M., & Müller, J. (2016). Mental health benefits of outdoor adventures: Results from two pilot studies. *Journal of Adolescence, 49,* 105–114. https://doi.org/10.1016/j. adolescence.2016.03.009

Perez, G. (2024, March 20). Applying an engineering education lens to today's socio-scientific/socio-technical realities: Public health, socioeconomic inequality, climate change, artificial intelligence and beyond [Symposium discussant]. 2024 NARST Annual International Conference, Denver, CO.

Pihkala, P. (2020). Anxiety and the ecological crisis: An analysis of eco-anxiety and climate anxiety. *Sustainability, 12*(19), 7836. https://doi.org/10.3390/su12197836

Regents of the University of California. (2023). What is sustainability? https://www. sustain.ucla.edu/what-is-sustainability/

Schutte, A. R., Torquati, J. C., & Beattie, H. L. (2017). Impact of urban nature on executive functioning in early and middle childhood. *Environment and Behavior, 49*(1), 3–30.

Smith, N., & Leiserowitz, A. (2014). The role of emotion in global warming policy support and opposition. *Risk Analysis, 34*(5), 937-948. https://doi.org/10.1111/ risa.12140

Sparkman, G., & Walton, G. M. (2017). Dynamic norms promote sustainable behaviour, even if it is counternormative. *Psychol. Sci.* 28, 1663–1674. https:// doi:10.1177/0956797617719950

Stephenson, M. E. (2013). Cosmic education. *NAMTA Journal, 38*(1), 119–132.

Stevenson, R. B. (2007). Schooling and environmental education: Contradictions in purpose and practice. *Environmental Education Research, 13*(2), 139–153. https://doi.org/10.1080/13504620701295726

Stevenson, K. T., Peterson, M. N., Bondell, H. D., Moore, S. E., & Carrier, S. J. (2014). Overcoming skepticism with education: Interacting influences of worldview and climate change knowledge on perceived climate change risk among adolescents. *Climatic Change, 126*, 293–304. https://doi.org/10.1007/s10584-014-1228-7

Thaler, R. H., & Sunstein, C. R. (2009). *Nudge: Improving decisions about health, wealth, and happiness.* Penguin Books.

United Nations. (2015, October 21). Transforming our world: The 2030 agenda for sustainable development. https://documents-dds-ny.un.org/doc/UNDOC/GEN/N15/291/89/PDF/N1529189.pdf?OpenElement

United Nations. (2023). The Sustainable development goals report 2023: Special edition-Towards a rescue plan for people and planet. https://unstats.un.org/sdgs/report/2023/The-Sustainable-Development-Goals-Report-2023.pdf

United Nations. (n.d.). Goal 17: Revitalize the global partnership for sustainable development. Sustainable Development Goals. https://www.un.org/sustainabledevelopment/globalpartnerships/#:~:text=It%20requires%20partnerships%20between%20governments,in%20our%20journey%20to%20development

United Nations Educational, Scientific and Cultural Organization (UNESCO). (2017). Education for sustainable development goals: Learning objectives. https://unesdoc.unesco.org/ark:/48223/pf0000247444

United Nations Educational, Scientific and Cultural Organization (UNESCO). (2020). Education for sustainable development: A roadmap. https://doi.org/10.54675/YFRE1448

United Nations Educational, Scientific and Cultural Organization (UNESCO). (n.d.). Education for sustainable development. https://www.unesco.org/en/sustainable-development/education#:~:text=UNESCO's%20ESD%20for%202030%20education,is%20necessary%20to%20change%20course

United States Department of Agriculture (USDA). (2023). *Food waste FAQ's.* https://www.usda.gov/foodwaste/faqs

University of Maryland Center for Environmental Science (UMCES). (2024). History of oysters. https://www.umces.edu/oysters/history#:~:text=In%20the%20early%2017th%20century,surface%2C%20sometimes%20becoming%20navigational%20hazards

Vandaele, M., & Stålhammar, S. (2022). "Hope dies, action begins?" The role of hope for proactive sustainability engagement among university students. *International Journal of Sustainability in Higher Education, 23*(8), 272–289. https://doi.org/10.1108/IJSHE-11-2021-0463

Virginia Institute of Marine Science (VIMS). (2024a). 'Catch the King' tide. https://www.vims.edu/people/loftis_jd/Catch%20the%20King/index.php

Virginia Institute of Marine Science (VIMS). (2024b). Marine advisory program. Chesapeake Bay National Estuarine Research Reserve (CBNERR). https://www.vims.edu/research/units/centerspartners/map/education/edworkgroup/cbnerr.php

Wilson, K. (2003). Therapeutic landscapes and First Nations peoples: An exploration of culture, health and place. *Health & Place, 9*(2), 83–93. https://doi.org/10.1016/S1353-8292(02)00016

Yang, Z. J., & Kahlor, L. (2013). What, me worry? The role of affect in information seeking and avoidance. *Science Communication, 35*(2), 189–212. https://doi.org/10.1177/1075547012441873

CHAPTER 7

Culturally Responsive Education: Fostering Equity and Social Justice in Montessori Education

By Sarah Hassebroek, EdS, Amira Mogaji, EdD, and Gabrielle Kotkov, MS

Key Terms:

Culturally Responsive Pedagogy: An approach to education that centers the knowledge of the communities in classrooms and uses the students' customs, traditions, experiences, and perspectives as tools for learning.

Diversity: The multiple characteristics of individual and group identities that should be valued. Including: race, ethnicity, gender, age, national origin, religion, ability, sexual orientation, socioeconomic status, language, and appearance. May also refer to ideas, perspectives, and values.

Eurocentrism: A worldview or mindset that centers European (or white) ways of knowing as superior to all others.

Ethnocentrism: A worldview or mindset that centers one culture (often Western European) and presents its ways of knowing as superior to all others.

Equity: To treat all fairly, with an emphasis on understanding and consideration of structural factors that benefit some and cause harm to others.

Intersectionality: Understanding that we hold multiple identities and that an individual can simultaneously hold identities of privilege and oppression. Kimberlé Crenshaw refers to the "prism" to look through and see the ways in which racism interacts with patriarchy, heterosexism, classism, and xenophobia.

Oppression: The systematic subjugation of a social group based on both power & prejudice of the advantaged group.

People of the Global Majority: An inclusive term that refers to the racial and ethnic groups that collectively make up the majority of the world's population, in favor of terms like "minorities."

Privilege: An unearned power or advantage, based on the formal and informal structures of a society.

Racism: Racial prejudice + social & institutional power; a system of advantage, based on race.

Restorative Justice: A justice theory that emphasizes repairing harm and collective accountability, placing decisions in the hands of the people most affected by the wrongdoing. Gives equal concern to the victim, the offender, and the surrounding community.

White Supremacy: The ideology that white people and their ideas, thoughts, and beliefs are superior to those of the People of the Global Majority. Also refers to the socio-economic system in which white people enjoy structural advantages and rights that other racial and ethnic groups do not, both at a collective and individual level.

Edited terms from Racial Equity Tools: https://www.racialequitytools.org/glossary

The foundations of the Montessori Method began from both a context of privilege and systemic disadvantage. Maria Montessori's path to obtaining a medical degree occurred when women were rarely represented in the medical field. Despite significant discrimination against women in leadership roles in medicine, Montessori persisted in obtaining her degree and becoming one of the first female doctors in Italy. What is not often noted is that she also had the privilege and a support system that allowed her to persevere through discriminatory circumstances to complete her degrees, enabling her to advocate for the rights of children in a time when children were typically meant to be seen and not heard.

Montessori also lived in a time of worldwide colonization (Mohandas, 2023). While it is undeniable that the macro-environment impacts the individual (Bronfenbrenner, 1977), Love argues that Montessori was a disruptor and "refused to live within the context of her time" (2023, p. 33). Understanding the context of Montessori education in the present day requires both a critical analysis of Maria Montessori's time and an understanding of how Eurocentrism, ethnocentrism, and white supremacy values undermine the goal of pedagogical equity that Dr. Montessori originally set out to achieve. By understanding our sociopolitical context, educators can prepare themselves to engage in action that fosters social awareness within the Montessori curriculum–action that is necessary to achieve the ideals of the Montessori Method.

The Montessori Method originated in the impoverished neighborhood of San Lorenzo in Rome, Italy, and focused on creating an inclusive environment to support all children. Maria Montessori was a social activist, aligning herself with the causes of women's rights, children's welfare, and educational reform (Moretti, 2021). While Montessori philosophy has its roots in pacifism and achieving world peace through education, many social justice issues still plague the Montessori education system. While individuals, organizations, and schools work tirelessly toward a more just and equitable future for Montessori educators and students, we must also strive to understand and impact our sociopolitical context to truly increase access to equitable education and provide a culturally relevant curriculum. The Montessori Movement encompasses both the Montessori Method and individual choices in implementing the method. Within the current political, social, and cultural pressures, the education system must continue to disrupt the status quo. This requires educators to examine and understand personal backgrounds and experiences. It also requires the willingness to critically examine resources, materials, policies, curricula, and assessments, and their impact on children, families, educators, and communities.

This chapter first discusses the responsibility of Montessori educators to engage in action that fosters equity and justice. Then, we share what it means to be a culturally responsive educator and provide actionable steps for educators regarding classroom materials, linguistic representation, access to Montessori education, social justice activism, and teacher education.

Equity, Justice, Accountability & Responsibility in the Classroom

Social justice education is defined as a community's effort to create a sustaining society based on equity values that are affirmed by that community. A social justice community endeavors to end systemic oppression and violence in the systems that work to devalue the dignity of others. Social justice education efforts recognize a legacy of past injustices and that the impacts of those past injustices remain in and around all of us. Therefore, renewed restorative justice efforts are needed to empower individuals and communities toward a shared understanding and effort for active change. Social justice education pushes the system to a new space that values all (John Lewis Institute for Social Justice, n.d.). The understanding of these justice efforts goes beyond humanity. In the Montessori theory, it is referred to as our cosmic task: "a way of seeing, a way of understanding the world" (Grazzini, 2013, p. 107). Montessori herself called us to care for all living creatures and for our planet.

When individual Montessori practitioners make choices for curriculum implementation, stories, or experiences to bring into the classroom, the work is guided by thoughtful reflection and consideration. Throughout history, there have been countless stories of resistance to systems of inequity. More often than not, these stories go untold, as the white supremacy movement actively works to cover and suppress social justice stories. Bell (2020) names the stories with colonial and white supremacy roots as Stock Stories. "Stock stories about race are strategic, operating to advance particular goals and interests." (Bell, 2020, p. 30). To understand a history beyond the limited history presented in textbooks, an overt effort must be made to understand other ways of knowing and being. Stock stories are estimated to comprise 90% of the curriculum, but only cover 1% of history (Bell, 2020). Oftentimes, real understanding comes through learning concealed stories from minoritized groups. "Articulation of these concealed stories is one of the sources of their survival, or 'survivance,' today" (Bell, 2020, p. 45). Becoming a part of the community we serve helps us be fluent and understand all students' background, language, culture, traditions—and stories (Ladson-Billings, 2009; Paris & Alim, 2014). Integrating educational justice practices into the classroom supports learners to feel seen and to be represented in their educational experiences. Below are a few examples of where we can dive deeper into these efforts, more can specifically be found throughout this text.

The pedagogical choices educators make have a rippling impact. These ripples can heal or cause harm to children, families, and communities. Therefore, school leaders and educators must work in community and in partnership with one another. Montessori's concept of whole child education is echoed by Erikson's concept of identity harmony, in which a child's realities are in harmony with their lived experience (Erikson, 1968). Working in this way supports learners and educators; mitigating teacher burnout and decreasing the number of teachers leaving the profession creates more stable schools, benefiting families, children, and communities (Iancu et. al, 2018).

Social Justice in Montessori Schools:
Culturally Responsive Pedagogy

Many Montessori programs, both public and private, strive and struggle to offer a culturally responsive approach, which can be defined as "an approach that promotes students' cultural strengths to support their well-being and achievement" (Debs & Brown, 2017, p. 2). Montessori pedagogy is well-situated to incorporate a culturally responsive curriculum, which allows and encourages teachers to bring aspects of their students' home cultures into their lessons (Debs & Brown, 2017). However, it is not enough to merely celebrate students' backgrounds; this provides just surface-level representation. Teachers also require education steeped in ABAR (anti-bias, anti-racist) teaching practices to examine their own implicit biases and create meaningful positive change in their classrooms and schools. Recent efforts from national and state organizations include additional requirements for integrated ABAR methods and professional development opportunities, including AMS.

A significant component of Montessori teacher training focuses on the preparation of the adult. A transformational process occurs within the teacher and involves the personal commitment to understanding one's own beliefs about children, and trusting the child. However, the process of transformation does not end with completing a teacher education program; it is ongoing work that also represents a commitment to social justice education. Engaging in an interrogation of self and social identity provides the framework for teachers to work towards dismantling oppressive beliefs and practices (Christensen, 2018; Foucault, 2010).

Maria Montessori believed that in order to serve students fully, the spiritual preparation of the teacher was more important than academic preparation. She wrote, "...the educator must prepare himself *inwardly*. He must examine himself methodically in order to discover certain defects that may become obstacles in his relation with the child" (Montessori, 1996, p. 89). While culturally responsive pedagogy provides a mechanism for educators to support the development of students' intellectual capacity, teachers' inability to translate culturally responsive pedagogical principles into practical application of culturally responsive teaching is a barrier rooted in both understanding and simultaneously implementing the key elements (Hammond, 2015). Ready for Rigor: A Framework for Culturally Responsive Teaching, developed by Dr. Zaretta Hammond, is a response to the observation that diverse students aren't given the type of robust instruction early on that builds their cognition (Hammond, 2018). Awareness, learning partnerships, information processing, and community building are the interconnected key elements in the Ready for Rigor framework (Hammond, 2015) and provide guidance and opportunities for reflection for school leaders and teachers engaging in effective culturally responsive teaching. It is important to note that two key components of the framework, awareness and learning partnerships, provide educators with the tools to identify the sociopolitical context of the students they serve, as well as their own sociopolitical position within that context.

Becoming a culturally responsive educator requires leaning into the discomfort of deep and purposeful reflection that acknowledges, accepts, and adjusts identified unconscious and implicit biases. In addition, cultural identity and personal beliefs directly impact personal interactions and relationships with students. Hammond (2015) suggests that in order to unearth implicit biases, teachers should identify their cultural frame of reference, recognize that their cultural lens impacts perception, and notice personal triggers. To improve and increase positive interactions and relationships with students, teachers may engage in practitioner action research that includes ongoing and continuous mindful reflection through a formalized process, and allows for elevating cultural frames of reference, inquiry of personal perceptions and assumptions, and plans for alternative responses (Dray & Wisneski, 2011; Hammond, 2015).

> **Becoming a culturally responsive educator requires leaning into the discomfort of deep and purposeful reflection that acknowledges, accepts, and adjusts identified unconscious and implicit biases.**

It is critical that discrimination never be present, observed, or tolerated when working with children. While becoming a practicing culturally responsive educator, it is important to not only monitor personal practices but also those of colleagues and family members/caregivers when necessary. Modeling the mindful reflection process and taking responsibility for any harm caused to students situates culturally responsive educators to become leaders for equity (Hammond, 2015).

Action Steps

- Share new ideas and practices used in class and with students
- Develop and nurture partnership relationships with families and caregivers
- Build an "equity muscle" to participate in discussions involving the topics of unconscious bias, race, class, and language
- Model and engage in asset-based conversations about students
- Form a school equity committee

Classroom Materials & Resources

A common misconception of the Montessori materials is that they are inherently unbiased, as they follow the child's developmental needs. However, many materials and resources in the classroom require a deeper study. Some examples include cultural studies, command cards, food preparation activities and snacks, books, and classroom decor.

Bishop (1990) describes the diversification with the metaphor of windows, doors, and mirrors. Books and materials can act as windows, mirrors, and doors to give children the opportunity to view other cultures or ways of being, reflect on their own cultures, or allow children to step into and experience cultures other than their own. Enriquez (2021) warns us to be critical of our interpretations of this concept and self-reflect to ensure that the mirrors are not so foggy that children cannot see themselves, the doors so heavy that they cannot open them on their own, or the windows too tiny or tall that they cannot see–or, in other words, ensure that the children can be independent in accessing the materials.

Action Steps

- See Chapter 3 for ideas and resources for preparing an environment that is culturally responsive and aligned with the Montessori philosophy.

Linguistic Representation

Children across the world are growing up in multilingual communities. In the United States, there are an estimated 51 million students in K–12 schools; an estimated 20–25% of these students are multilingual, speaking more than 400 languages. Approximately 10% of these learners are enrolled in English-language programs (National Center for Education Statistics, 2023). Approximately 15 million children are multilingual (Statista, 2023). Despite the large number of multilingual learners, monolingualism persists in American school systems. This is not accidental; it is by design. "White ideologies of normalcy" (Dover & Rodríguez-Valls, 2022), which name what is "normal" or "abnormal," seep into the languages, accents, and expressions allowed within the walls of the school building. Paris describes a pedagogy that works towards positive social transformation and honors an additive, rather than deficit view and an emancipatory vision for education: culturally sustaining pedagogy (2012). "Culturally sustaining pedagogy (CSP), builds off of Culturally Responsive Pedagogy, is a critical framework for centering and sustaining Indigenous, Black, Latinx, Asian and Pacific Islander communities as these memberships necessarily intersect with gender and sexuality, dis/ability, class, language, land and more" (Alim et al., 2022). Regarding linguistic representation, centering multilingualism as a core component of a school's identity is a way to uphold CSP. Battery Park Montessori, a trilingual Montessori program in New York, is one good example.

Modeling and encouraging interlanguage practice in the classroom allows learners to make connections between languages and strengthen their understanding of all languages while avoiding frustration. Translanguaging, the practice of using multiple languages together fluidly, "recognizes that the development of proficiency in one language cannot reasonably be separated from other languages" (Fu et al., 2019, p. 7). Montessori practitioners can support students' multiple identities and languages and cultural pluralism by modeling and implementing the following practices.

Action Steps

- Explore the languages that exist in your school and community.

- Invite and encourage children to use any language in writing and choose the word that best fits their meaning.

- Model and encourage individual language use that amplifies and expands the collective linguistic repertoire.

- Pre-teach vocabulary to support all emergent learners.

- Provide sentence frames to reduce cognitive load when applying new vocabulary.

- Facilitate peer networks to support vocabulary development and practice.

- Explore resources available in your school and local library.

- Plan important communications that are commonly sent (no-school days, field trips, etc.), and translate letters for families so that all families receive communications at the same time.

- Engage in continued reflection on the dynamic and ever-shifting nature of the community.

Access to Montessori

While public Montessori schools offer increased access to Montessori education, they face challenges in their ability to offer a diverse teaching staff and maintain a diverse student population (Debs & Brown, 2017). Like the nationwide public school teacher population, public Montessori school educators are overwhelmingly white and female, which can lead to feelings of isolation and marginalization among Montessori teachers of color (Debs & Brown, 2017). Public Montessori programs have been found to have many benefits for students of color, including minimizing racially disproportionate discipline and limiting overidentification for special education. Still, they can struggle to maintain diverse enrollments, especially when parents are required to research their choices, navigate complicated enrollment systems, and sometimes provide transportation to and from school (Debs & Brown, 2017). Many Montessori programs exist in private programming centers. The cost of tuition varies greatly by region and is $12,350 on average in 2023 (Hanson, 2023). Although scholarship programs are available, private programs often create a barrier for families to enroll their children. Ayer (2016) highlights innovative private schools that are making efforts to offer tuition assistance through "tuition-based, access-oriented" programs.

Although the Method seeks to create classroom environments that reflect the families and children they serve, more often than not, access to Montessori teacher training requires a financial and monetary commitment that is out of reach for many. An aspect of social justice that Montessori education continues to contend with are issues of access and affordability. Only approximately 9% of Montessori schools worldwide are government-funded (Debs et al., 2022). Although the United States is among the top four countries worldwide with the highest number of public Montessori programs (Debs et al., 2022), as little as 10% of the 5,000 Montessori schools in the United States are public schools (American Montessori Society, 2023). Many of these are concentrated in urban areas, and thus, geography becomes a barrier to access. (Please see Chapter 4 for more on access and social justice in public Montessori programs). Virtual Montessori programs, which experienced a boom at the start of the COVID-19 pandemic, attempt to address the problem of geographic access to Montessori education; however, they do not solve the problem of affordability, as most are privately funded (Kotkov, 2022). Although financial aid is often offered, participating families are still required to have access to a computer or tablet for their child's use, a stable internet connection, and an adult present at home, making it financially unavailable to many families (Kotkov, 2022). In making pedagogical decisions, school leadership teams should remain in conversation with the community they serve to understand their needs and evaluate the accessibility of their programs.

Action Steps:

- Advocate to local school boards

- Invite legislators to visit classrooms or school events

- Explore pathways to teacher licensure in your state

- For additional information, see the National Center for Montessori in the Public Sector (public-montessori.org) and the Montessori Public Policy Initiative (montessoriadvocacy.org).

Social Justice Activism & Advocacy

Social justice advocacy at the macro level to support funding, programming, and the teaching profession (Fenech & Lotz, 2018) is defined as "systems advocacy." In contrast, micro-advocacy encompasses the daily work to contextualize the needs of the individual in the classroom and the daily choices that support individual children's needs. "It is essential that preservice teachers acquire the skills necessary to become leaders in advocating for CLD (culturally and linguistically diverse) students and families" (Holmes & Herrera, 2009, p. 204).

The 2013 founding of Montessori for Social Justice (MSJ) as a social justice Montessori advocacy and activism organization was a direct response to the need for those Montessorians who had a "personal commitment to public Montessori and social justice" to have access to not only each other but also to relevant resources to support their individual and collective advocacy efforts (MSJ website, n.d.). Montessori for Social Justice continues to uphold their organizational mission: "We support the creation of sustainable learning environments that dismantle systems of oppression, amplify voices of the Global Majority, and cultivate partnerships to liberate the human potential " (MSJ website, n.d.). Consequently, since its inception, MSJ has expanded its impact, from creating a centralized listserv to connect like-minded Montessorians and share equity resources to becoming one of the leaders in equity and social justice-focused professional development through conferences and webinars within the Montessori community.

Social justice advocacy efforts can be the primary focus of a Montessori organization (as with MSJ, for example), but more often are one integral component of an organization. For example, in 2018, the American Montessori Society board of directors voted to include equity and inclusion as an organizational strategic priority (AMS, n.d.). Creating a standing board committee for justice, equity, diversity, and inclusion (JEDI) and the AMS Diversity, Equity, & Inclusion Scholarship are direct byproducts of this equity and inclusion strategic priority. They reflect the organization's commitment to creating access to professional development opportunities for people who identify as members of marginalized and under-resourced populations. They also address the needs of those working in and leading Montessori teacher education programs and schools that support disenfranchised and under-resourced student populations (AMS, n.d.); ultimately, these measures will ensure equitable and inclusive environments for all students.

Action Steps:

- Support current efforts and organizations through donations, attending events, and sharing information with colleagues.

- If there is no local network, consider starting a local group for equity and social justice.

- Start an Equity committee in your building to evaluate efforts to achieve equity, meet the needs of your children, families, and community, and center their voices.

Teacher Education Programs

The accessibility and affordability of high-quality Montessori teacher education programs is another social justice issue within the community. Montessori training can be prohibitively expensive for prospective Montessori educators, regardless of background. In addition, the training methods are often offered in the form of lectures and are rooted in Eurocentric views of teaching and assessing learning. For more on Montessori teacher education, see Chapter 9.

Montessori teacher education programs continue to engage in efforts to diversify teaching staff; these efforts are necessary but insufficient to change systemic inequities meaningfully. In addition, programs are integrating anti-bias and culturally responsive curricula, and examining their curricula, policies, and practices with a critical lens. Several organizations and training programs, including Black Montessori Education Fund and KCLC's Indigenous Montessori Institute, are working to diversify the pool of Montessori teachers by increasing outreach and funding for Montessori training for teachers of color..

Affordable and accessible teacher education programs are the first steps towards creating social justice-oriented Montessori teacher training. Many educators of color have found Montessori teacher training programs are centered on whiteness, with little emphasis on culturally responsive curriculum and ABAR teaching practices (D'Cruz Ramos, 2023). While many Montessori teacher education programs and organizations have incorporated ABAR principles into their programs, not all Montessori accreditations require this content. Several programs, including The Barrie Institute for Advanced Montessori Studies, led by director Hilary Green, proactively created space for ABAR experiences for adult learners as they worked to embed ABAR training into the program (AMS, 2023, p. 40). In 2022, the American Montessori Society board of directors voted to include 12 credits of ABAR training as a requirement for AMS-affiliated teacher education programs (TEPs) by 2023. An additional resource for TEPs is *Equity Examined: How to Design Schools and Teacher Education Programs Where Everyone Thrives* (AMS, 2023), which not only includes essays from the field but also provides equity assessment tools, reflective questions, and additional resources for TEPs, schools, classrooms, and teachers.

Montessori teacher education has traditionally prepared teachers to work in private programs, which make up the majority of Montessori schools in the United States (Debs & Brown, 2017). A program trying to bridge this gap and prepare educators for teaching in public schools is the DC Montessori Teacher Residency Program, which incorporates topics such as cultural competency, family engagement, and support for English-language learners into the curriculum (Debs & Brown, 2017). Support for non-English speaking teachers in training is also an issue facing Montessori teacher education programs. Some AMI training programs outside of the United States offer bilingual or multilingual support for students by involving multiple trainers with different language backgrounds or with the use of an interpreter (Feez & Morgan, 2023). While this can open up lecture content to cultural interpretation and potentially change the intended meaning, it offers access to Montessori training to adults of different linguistic backgrounds and, possibly more importantly, fights the "monolingual mindset" and affirms individuals from non-dominant cultures (Feez & Morgan, 2023). Teacher education must include the guidance and support of students to question their pedagogy, the institutional inequalities, racism, and the injustice that exists both in education and society (Ladson-Billings, 2009).

Action Steps:

- Advocate to your Montessori teacher educator program (TEP) to ask for additional training and professional development on equity topics that are important to your community.

- Donate to scholarships for teachers of the Global Majority.

- Contact your TEP and invite them to allow observers in your classroom community.

- Advocate to state and non-profit organizations for additional funding or access to grants for Montessori training.

Conclusion

To achieve the social liberation of the child, we must create and nurture an educational system that meets children's developmental and academic needs in a culturally sustainable manner.

Maria Montessori advocated for the liberation of the child, and these efforts continue today. The movement for social justice is dynamic, adapting in both individual and systemic efforts. To achieve the social liberation of the child, we must create and nurture an educational system that meets children's developmental and academic needs in a culturally sustainable manner. Without these efforts, the "oppressive reality absorbs those within it" (Freire, 1970, p. 51). The work toward an anti-oppressive and peaceful society follows Dr. Montessori's intentions for the Method; it cannot be done in isolation. Social justice efforts enacted in community through collaboration and collective action can bring the ideals of the Montessori Method to fruition.

Discussion Questions

- In what ways are you a culturally responsive educator?

- What does social justice activism look like for you? On a micro level? On a macro level?

- Did your teacher education program include ABAR content or requirements? If not, what might you do to commit to social justice in your Montessori pedagogy?

References

Alim, H. S., Paris, D., & Wong, C. P. (2022). Culturally sustaining pedagogy: A critical framework for centering communities. In (Eds. Suad-Nasir, N., Lee, C., Pea, R., & McKinney de Royston, M.), *Handbook of the cultural foundations of learning* (pp. 261–276). Routledge.

Ayer, D. (2016). Public, private, or something in between? A new model for Montessori schools. *Montessori Public*. https://www.montessoripublic. org/2016/10/3414/

American Montessori Society (AMS). (n.d.). *Fast facts: Public Montessori schools*. Montessori resources for schools, teachers, families and parents. https://amshq.org/ About-AMS/Press-kit/Public-Schools

American Montessori Society (AMS). (n.d.). *AMS diversity, equity, & inclusion scholarship program*. https://amshq.org/About-AMS/Donate/DEI-Scholarship-Fund

American Montessori Society. (2023). Equity examined: How to design schools and teacher education programs where everyone thrives. American Montessori Society.

Bell, L. A. (2020). *Storytelling for social justice: Connecting narrative and the arts in anti-racist teaching*. (Second ed.). Routledge.

Bishop, R. S. (1990, March). Windows and mirrors: Children's books and parallel cultures. In California State University reading conference: 14th annual conference proceedings (pp. 3–12).

Bronfenbrenner, U. (1977). Toward an experimental ecology of human development. *American Psychologist, 32*(7), 513.

Christensen, O. (2018). *Transforming the transformation: A post-intentional phenomenological exploration of Montessori teachers engaging in anti-bias and anti-racist teacher self-reflection*. (Dissertation) University of Minnesota.

D'Cruz Ramos, G. O. (2023). Critical Montessori education: Centering BIPOC Montessori educators and their anti-racist teaching practices (Dissertation). Retrieved from https://www.proquest.com/openview/ ff1a9e8e750b23bda2b4803cdbf87ae3/1?pq-origsite=gscholar&cbl=18750&diss=y

Debs, M. C., & Brown, K. E. (2017). Students of color and Public Montessori schools: A review of the literature. *Journal of Montessori Research, 3*(1), 1. https://doi. org/10.17161/jomr.v3i1.5859

Debs, M. C., De Brouwer, J., Murray, A. K., Lawrence, L., Tyne, M., & Von der Wehl, C. (2022). Global diffusion of Montessori schools. *Journal of Montessori Research, 8*(2), 1–15. https://doi.org/10.17161/jomr.v8i2.18675

Dray, B., & Wisneski, D. (2011). Mindful reflection as a process for developing culturally responsive practices. *Teaching Exceptional Children, 44*(1), 28–36. https://doi.org.10.1177/00400599104400104

Dover, A., & Rodríguez-Valls, F. (2022). *Radically inclusive teaching with newcomer and emergent plurilingual students: Braving up.* Teachers College Press.

Enriquez, G. (2021). Foggy mirrors, tiny windows, and heavy doors: Beyond diverse books toward meaningful literacy instruction. *The Reading Teacher, 75*(1), 103–106.

Erikson, E. H. (1968). *Identity: Youth and crisis.* W.W. Norton.

Feez, S., & Morgan, A.-M. (2023). Montessori education in a plurilingual World. In *The Bloomsbury Handbook of Montessori Education* (1st ed., pp. 489–501). Bloomsbury Publishing.

Fenech, M., & Lotz, M. (2018). Systems advocacy in the professional practice of early childhood teachers: From the antithetical to the ethical. *Early Years, 38*(1), 19–34.

Freire, P. (1970). *Pedagogy of the oppressed.* Continuum International Publishing Group.

Foucault, M. (2010). Truth and power. In P. Rabinow (Ed.) *The Foucault Reader* (pp. 51–76). Random House. (Original published work 1977)

Fu, D., Hadjioannou, X., & Zhou, X. (2019). *Translanguaging for emergent bilinguals: Inclusive teaching in the linguistically diverse classroom.* Teachers College Press.

Grazzini, C. (2013). Maria Montessori's cosmic vision, cosmic plan, and cosmic education. *NAMTA Journal, 38*(1), 107–116.

Hammond, Z. (2015). *Culturally responsive teaching & the brain: Promoting authentic engagement and rigor among culturally and linguistically diverse students.* Corwin.

Hammond, Z. (2018). Culturally responsive teaching puts rigor at the center: Q&A with Zaretta Hammond. *Learning Professional, 39*(5), 40–43. https://learningforward.org/wp-content/uploads/2018/10/culturally-responsive-teaching-puts-rigor-at-the-center.pdf

Hanson, M. (2023). Average cost of private school. Education Data. https://educationdata.org/average-cost-of-private-school

Holmes, M., & Herrera, S., (2009). Enhancing advocacy skills of teacher candidates. *Teaching Education, 20*(2)., pp. 203–213.

Iancu, A. E., Rusu, A., Maroiu, C., Pacurar, R., & Maricutoiu, L. P. (2018). The effectiveness of interventions aimed at reducing teacher burnout: A meta-analysis. *Education*

Psychological Review, 30, pp. 373–396. https://link.springer.com/article/10.1007/s10648-017-9420-8

John Lewis Institute for Social Justice. (n.d.). *Our definition of social justice.* Central Connecticut State University. https://www.ccsu.edu/john-lewis-institute-social-justice/our-definition-social-justice

Kotkov, G. (2022). Virtualizing Montessori : Experiences of teachers working in a fully remote Montessori preschool (Dissertation). Retrieved from https://urn.kb.se/resolve?urn=urn:nbn:se:liu:diva-186887

Ladson-Billings, G. (2009). *The dreamkeepers: Successful teachers of African American children (2nd ed).* Jossey-Bass.

Love, K. (2023). Maria Montessori was a rebel. *Montessori Life, 32–34.*

Mohandas, S. (2023). Transforming practice: A critical interrogation of Montessori. *Montessori Life, 35–40.*

Montessori, M. (1996). *The secret of childhood.* Orient Blackswan Private Limited.

Montessori for Social Justice. (n.d.). *Montessori for social justice: About us.* http://www.montessoriforsocialjustice.org/about/

Moretti, E. (2021). *The best weapon for peace: Maria Montessori, education, and children's rights.* The University of Wisconsin Press.

National Center for Education Statistics. (2023). Public school enrollment. https://nces.ed.gov/programs/coe/indicator/cga

Paris, D. (2012). Culturally sustaining pedagogy: A needed change in stance, terminology, and practice. *Educational Researcher, 41*(3), 93–97.

Paris, D., & Alim, H. S. (2014). What are we seeking to sustain through culturally sustaining pedagogy? A loving critique forward. *Harvard Educational Review, 84*(1), 85–100.

Statista. (2023). Number of children who speak another language than English at home in the United States from 1979–2019. https://www.statista.com/statistics/476745/number-of-children-who-speak-another-language-than-english-at-home-in-the-us/

CHAPTER 8

Family Engagement in Montessori Schools in the U.S. and China: A Cross-Cultural Exploration

By Martha Teien, MEd, and Jesmine Lok

Maria Montessori developed a method of education focused on relationships—relationships between the student, the teacher, and the environment. She emphasized this "trinity" throughout her writings (Lillard & McHugh, 2019, p. 19). While the Montessori trinity does not emphasize family-teacher collaboration as a central component, Montessori highlighted the significance of the child's environment, including home and school, in shaping their development (Montessori, 1967, p. 89). She underscored the need for collaboration between families[9] and educators to create a nurturing environment that supports the child's natural curiosity, independence, and love of learning. Her foregrounding of family-teacher relationships is now confirmed through research that shows quality family-teacher relationships support children's academic and behavioral outcomes (Garbacz et al., 2016; Minke et al., 2014) and can be strengthened through family-school engagement and collaboration (e.g., Garbacz et al., 2016). Finding a balance between the Montessori focus on the student/teacher

---

9 We use the terms *family, families, caregivers,* and *guardians* in this chapter to refer to any primary caregiver or guardian of a child, whether biologically related or not, to recognize the diversity of adults in children's lives.

relationship and incorporating family engagement into the educational process can better support families and improve student outcomes.

To explore the extent of family involvement in schools, the Programme for International Student Assessment (PISA), which assesses and compares the performance of education systems worldwide, surveyed school principals in 38 countries. They were asked to report the percentage of parents who engaged in specific school-related events in the previous academic year. The survey found that China's (Beijing, Shanghai, Jiangsu, and Zhejiang) family engagement rate is significantly higher than that of the United States across four school activities (OECD, 2019). These activities encompassed independent discussions initiated by parents regarding their child's progress with teachers, discussions initiated by teachers themselves about the child's progress, involvement in local school governance, and volunteering in physical or extracurricular activities. China is also estimated to have one of the world's largest number of Montessori schools, with approximately 1,000 schools, and is growing rapidly (Debs et al., 2023; Whitescarver & Cossentino, 2008).

We contend that regardless of where a Montessori school is located, the Montessori approach benefits from a stronger emphasis on family-teacher relationships, particularly when open lines of communication between teachers and caregivers are promoted, information about Montessori's guiding principles and practical applications is disseminated, and culturally relevant teaching is prioritized.

At the same time, in today's dynamic educational landscape in China, Montessori preschools face various challenges. Among these challenges are navigating stringent regulatory requirements, competing with publicly funded alternatives, and promoting parental and family awareness and acceptance of Montessori education. This chapter explores family engagement in Montessori schools in the United States and China. We contend that regardless of where a Montessori school is located, the Montessori approach benefits from a stronger emphasis on family-teacher relationships, particularly when open lines of communication between teachers and caregivers are promoted, information about Montessori's guiding principles and practical applications is disseminated, and culturally relevant teaching is prioritized. In the following sections, we share what family and school partnerships look like in practice by outlining challenges and opportunities. We focus on how Montessori practitioners in the U.S. and China may learn from each other to improve family engagement and collaboration. By improving family involvement and support in Montessori education, cross-cultural training and collaborative research projects can enhance practices and outcomes in both countries, helping Montessori education to advance globally.

Family-School Partnerships in Practice: Challenges and Opportunities

The educational journey in both countries involves much more than the academic content delivered within classroom walls. Students bring many experiences, backgrounds, and personal circumstances that influence their learning processes and outcomes. A solid family-teacher bond fosters trust and collaboration and enhances the child's educational experience. It allows caregivers to understand their child's strengths, weaknesses, and progress, enabling them to provide targeted support and reinforcement at home. Moreover, when families and teachers work together as partners, they can collectively address any challenges or concerns, leading to a more holistic and successful educational journey for the student.

Family and school partnerships can take many forms, including families discussing education with their child, assisting with homework, watching their child's educational progress, talking with school employees, engaging in decision-making, and participating in school activities (LaRocque et al., 2011). While relationships between families and educators are similar in China and the United States, priorities may differ. For example, in the U.S., there is a strong emphasis on personalized education plans through Individualized Education Programs (IEPs) and active participation in parent-teacher associations (PTAs), which organize events and provide additional resources for families. Many U.S. families also prioritize assisting children with homework and encouraging involvement in extracurricular activities to support holistic development. In China, families may prioritize academic achievement and exam preparation, such as the Gaokao (National Higher Education Entrance Examination, the standardized college entrance exam in China), and often invest in supplementary education like tutoring. A traditional emphasis on respecting authority, including teachers, influences interactions with schools. Despite these differences, both societies value open communication between families and schools, parental involvement in children's education, and supporting holistic development, albeit with varying emphases and cultural nuances.

Cross-cultural collaboration and sharing best practices can enhance strategies and foster stronger partnerships with families in both China and the U.S. Utilizing a global perspective to strengthen family engagement with Montessori schools might include collaborative training programs and joint research projects.

Epstein et al. (2019) suggest six recommendations for collaboration between families and schools: 1) guardian knowledge and skills, 2) communicating between home and school, 3) volunteering at school and in the community, 4) supporting student learning at home, 5) involvement in decision-making and advocacy, and 6) collaborating with the community. We take these recommendations a step further and combine research with examples of family and teacher collaborations to share opportunities and challenges of family-teacher partnerships in practice in the United States and China.

Communication Between Home and School

Strong communication between home and school is crucial for students' holistic development and academic success. Parents and educators can collaboratively support a child's learning journey by maintaining open and effective communication channels. Regular updates on a student's progress, both academically and socially, allow parents to intervene early if issues arise. Moreover, ongoing dialogue makes understanding a child's unique needs and strengths possible, enabling educators to tailor teaching strategies accordingly. For parents, being informed about school policies, curriculum changes, and upcoming events fosters a sense of partnership and involvement in their child's education. Ultimately, a unified approach between home and school creates a supportive environment where students feel valued, motivated, and encouraged to reach their full potential academically and personally.

Goonetilleke (2021) examined the interactions between educators and families in a U.S. Montessori school setting and identified how families engaged in Montessori Early Childhood educational environments. The findings indicated that communication by email or newsletter and social gatherings strengthened the partnerships between home and educators. A shared leadership method incorporates all perspectives into decision-making, ensuring families' and educators' opinions are considered, and solutions to foster children's development are effectively implemented. The challenges to these recommendations were the time availability for the families and the school, including the increased time commitment required from both parties for detailed written communications and participating in social events outside school hours.

In China, researchers interviewed two private Montessori heads of schools and learned that ongoing communication between parents and Montessori teachers was maintained using typical social networking platforms such as WeChat video channels and live webinars (Wang & Zhao, 2019). As a result of using a typical social networking platform, parents and teachers can communicate openly and transparently. As part of the social media platform, "we post important announcements and updates, organize virtual parent-teacher meetings, and provide parents with educational materials and resources that will help them support their child at home and communicate important announcements and updates" (Wang & Zhao, 2019). Using a common social platform to communicate with parents has significantly increased parental involvement in these Montessori schools. If parents are provided with a convenient and accessible platform for communication, they will be better able to stay informed about and engaged in their children's learning process. By doing so, "we will be able to strengthen the parent-teacher bond and empower parents to take more active steps towards supporting their child's educational success at home as well as strengthen the parent-teacher relationship" (Wang & Zhao, 2019).

Family Knowledge of Montessori Practices and Pedagogy

Consistency between Montessori practices at home and school can often be challenging, particularly when it comes to educating families on the underlying principles and philosophies that guide this unique educational model. One of the primary challenges in this regard is the contrast between the Montessori approach and the non-Montessori educational model that many families have experienced in their academic journey. For example, Montessori schools typically do not include homework, which can sometimes worry parents who were taught that educational achievement is closely tied to the amount of time dedicated to schoolwork outside the classroom. Many parents are more familiar with what Paulo Freire called the banking system of education—"an approach where the teacher deposits information into students who passively receive it" (Freire et al., 2018, p. 71). Maria Montessori observed a natural desire to learn that encourages a child to fall in love with learning. The Method's emphasis on fostering independence and self-directed learning can be perceived as an unfamiliar risk due to the departure from the teacher-directed approaches commonly found in non-Montessori educational settings.

In Montessori education, independence is a cornerstone principle that empowers children to take ownership of their learning process and develop essential life skills. When families understand the significance of independence in learning and implement these practices at home, they contribute significantly to their children's academic growth and personal development. Encouraging independence helps children learn responsibility by managing their tasks independently and building self-discipline through focused, self-directed work. It also fosters critical thinking skills as children are encouraged to explore solutions and make decisions autonomously. This approach enhances academic performance and nurtures children's confidence, initiative, and resilience, preparing them for future challenges.

Since Montessori schools encourage independent learning, they often do not assign homework or give out letter grades, making it challenging for families to monitor their children's educational progress or compare assignments. As a result, families may feel frustrated about their role and be less engaged with their school. These frustrated feelings can be addressed by utilizing regular communication and creating a culture of transparency (Lillard, 2005). Community events like parent education nights or community dinners (Jessen, 2010) can allow for informal settings where the school setting becomes a resource for understanding the philosophy, and the signs of educational progress can be viewed from different lenses.

The Montessori philosophy's focus on independence can result in limited family presence in classrooms/on school grounds; many Montessori schools require guardians to drop off and pick up their children in a parking lot or outside school gates. The rationale behind limiting guardian presence in classrooms is deeply rooted in the educational objectives of fostering children's independence, concentration, social development, and self-efficacy. It is not about excluding families from the educational process but rather about creating the best conditions for children's growth and learning. However, this practice can make it challenging to foster strong family-school collaboration and leave guardians feeling disconnected from their children (Ling Koh & Frick, 2010). Social independence is an essential factor in creating a safe, happy transition, and it is an important role that families can assist with before ever arriving at the school, by setting the stage for this independence. This parental action can be essential in tying together the two environments, and schools can thank parents for this effort, acknowledging that their support is the glue for the evolution of collaboration.

A 2015 study in the United States examined Montessori Early Childhood teachers' perceptions of family stressors and priorities, finding a significant difference in the families' priorities and what the teachers assumed family priorities to be. Teachers assumed the families valued "making academic progress"; in fact, the families' top priority was "developing kindness" in their children (Epstein, 2015). Both families and teachers identified that the number one family stressor was "insufficient time." At the same time, the cultural emphasis on academic achievement and success in China may lead some parents to prioritize traditional education methods over the Montessori philosophy, further complicating the process of parental involvement. The traditional Chinese educational system also emphasizes academic achievement and standardized testing, which leads to a need for more understanding and appreciation of Montessori education's holistic approach and child-centered nature.

Promoting parental awareness and acceptance of Montessori education in China can significantly benefit from school-organized workshops or informational sessions, and collaborating with local community centers. These efforts aim to educate parents about Montessori principles, highlighting its child-centered approach, hands-on learning, and the prepared environment's role. Workshops can feature Montessori educators, psychologists, and experienced parents who provide insights and engage in interactive Q&A sessions and practical demonstrations. Hosting open houses allows parents to observe Montessori classrooms in action, participate in live demonstrations of Montessori materials, and meet teachers and parents, offering a firsthand experience of the Montessori Method's effectiveness. Collaborating with local community centers and organizations can expand outreach, creating a supportive network that introduces Montessori concepts through educational fairs, parenting seminars, and children's activity days. Research underscores the positive impact of active parental involvement in education, with studies showing that effective family-school partnerships lead to improved student outcomes and a positive school climate. Examples of successful programs, such as family nights and parent education series in Montessori schools, demonstrate how these initiatives can strengthen the home-school connection. In China, similar approaches have shown promising results, increasing parental support and enrollment in Montessori programs. By combining these strategies with robust research and practical examples, efforts to promote Montessori education in China can become more effective, leading to greater parental acceptance and awareness (Epstein, 2011; Henderson & Mapp, 2002; Lillard, 2005; Li & Chen, 2019).

Culturally Responsive/Relevant Frameworks

An educator must recognize the whole child as an extension of their family and culture. As author bell hooks (1994) wrote, "... my teachers made sure they 'knew' us. They knew our parents, our economic status, where we worshipped, what our homes were like, and how we were treated in the family" (p. 3). Culturally relevant pedagogy (CRP) is one way to get to know the whole child and their family, as it incorporates curricula that reflect the cultural backgrounds of children and their families. The roots of CRP come from the U.S. civil rights movement

(Ladson-Billings, 1995) and have grown to become a part of contemporary educational theory to create more effective learning environments (Hammond, 2015). For example, Byrd (2016) examined the impacts of CRP on students' academic outcomes and ethnic-racial identity development. Surveys garnered responses from 315 sixth – through twelfth-grade students of various races from all over the United States. CRP utilized in racially diverse student populations was found to enhance academic engagement, foster positive racial identities, and support intercultural understanding. Further, researchers at the University of Virginia conducted a mixed-methods study on Montessori as a culturally relevant pedagogy (Lillard et al., 2021). Their findings robustly indicate that Montessori's emphasis on self-determination, academic excellence, and empowerment aligns, in theory and practice, with the principles of equity and excellence that are the bedrock of a culturally responsive pedagogy.

Professional Standards and Competencies of Early Childhood Educators is a position statement released by The National Association for the Education of Young Children (NAEYC) in 2020. In the document, the organization recommends that teachers: "(a) know about, understand, and value the diversity in family characteristics. Early childhood educators (b) use this understanding to create respectful, responsive, reciprocal relationships with families and to engage with them as partners in their young children's development and learning" (p. 12). Derman-Sparks and Edwards (2019) coined the four core goals of anti-bias education, which offer children "the skills of empowerment and the ability to stand up for themselves or others." The first goal is identity: "a strong sense of individual and group identities is the foundation for the three other core anti-bias goals," which are diversity, justice, and activism.

The child's first sense of identity is their physical sense, based on sensory experience. Over time, the environments and people around them help form their identity, and NAEYC encourages teachers to "nurture each child's construction of knowledgeable, confident, individual personal and social identities" (Derman-Sparks & Edwards, 2019). This is where families can substantially communicate their social norms, beliefs, and values to their child's teacher. Montessori philosophy places high value on identity and creates classrooms where personal and social identities flourish: "The student-centered approach of Montessori philosophy promotes autonomy, cooperation, and student voice, helping students develop self-confidence as they contribute their ideas, thoughts, and feelings" (White, 2023). Multi-year/mixed-age classrooms also serve the purpose of a deeper relationship between student/family and teacher, allowing the guide a better sense of the child's personal and family identities.

Dr. Montessori honored the depth and importance of the family-child and teacher-child relationships, even though she did not write explicitly on family-teacher partnerships. However, if we pair the research above with Montessori's philosophy, we have good foundational information on collaborating with families. To create a supportive and effective learning environment that respects and builds on the strengths of each student's unique cultural heritage, Montessori guides must recognize the varied backgrounds and experiences that students bring to the classroom. Open lines of communication and collaboration with families to fully understand each student's needs, values, and expectations support the guide's efforts. Chinese cultural values include incorporating elements of Confucianism, such as respect for elders and emphasis on harmony, into the classroom environment. Educators can create a harmonious and respectful learning environment by incorporating elements of Confucianism into the Montessori classroom. Emphasizing respect for elders can foster a culture of reverence and appreciation for authority figures while promoting harmony and peace education, encouraging students to develop strong interpersonal skills and resolve conflicts peacefully. These values align with the Montessori philosophy of promoting social and emotional development, creating a well-rounded educational experience that integrates Chinese cultural norms and the principles of Montessori education.

Additionally, incorporating traditional Chinese arts, calligraphy, and tea ceremony activities into the curriculum can help children connect with their cultural heritage while benefiting from the Montessori approach to learning. Finally, fostering a sense of community and collective responsibility within the classroom can align with the values of collectivism and cooperation that are prominent in Chinese culture.

CHAPTER 8

A Path Forward

Recapping Opportunities and Challenges

Family engagement in Montessori schools presents numerous opportunities to enhance the educational experience for children. One significant opportunity is the potential for creating a strong home-school connection, where parents are deeply involved in their child's learning process. This engagement allows parents to understand and reinforce Montessori principles at home, fostering a consistent learning environment beyond the classroom. Additionally, Montessori schools can leverage family engagement to build a supportive community that contributes to a positive school culture and enhances student well-being and academic success.

Moreover, involving parents in school activities and decision-making processes empowers them to contribute their unique skills and perspectives, enriching the school environment. This collaboration can lead to innovative solutions and initiatives that benefit the entire school community. Research shows that active parental involvement is linked to improved student outcomes, including higher academic achievement, better social skills, and increased motivation. Therefore, fostering family engagement is beneficial and essential for maximizing Montessori education's potential.

Despite these opportunities, several challenges can hinder effective family engagement in Montessori schools. One primary challenge is the need for more understanding of and familiarity with Montessori principles among parents. Many parents may come from traditional educational backgrounds, and might initially need help to grasp the Montessori Method's distinct approaches, such as the emphasis on self-directed learning and the mixed-age classrooms. This gap in understanding can lead to misconceptions and hesitations about fully embracing Montessori philosophy.

Another significant challenge is the diverse range of family dynamics and circumstances. Parents' availability and capacity to engage with the school can vary widely due to factors such as work schedules, socioeconomic status, and language

135

barriers. These disparities can make creating inclusive engagement strategies that effectively cater to all families challenging. Additionally, schools may need more support in organizing regular and meaningful engagement activities, further complicating efforts to maintain consistent and impactful family involvement.

Montessori schools remain a great place for families to become engaged in meaningful ways. Schools can offer comprehensive orientation programs and regular workshops to bridge the understanding gap and educate parents about Montessori principles and practices. Clear communication channels and resource access will help parents feel more confident and informed about their child's education. A stronger partnership between the school and the family will result in a better student learning environment.

To address the diverse needs of families, schools can implement flexible and varied engagement strategies, such as virtual meetings, multilingual resources, and community partnerships that support working parents and those from different socioeconomic backgrounds. Creating a welcoming and inclusive atmosphere ensures every family feels valued and supported; if schools can foster a sense of belonging, they can create an environment where all families feel heard and represented. This can be achieved through culturally responsive practices, a curriculum that reflects different backgrounds, and ongoing communication that celebrates the unique contributions of each family.

Discussion Questions

- How can Montessori schools effectively bridge the gap in families' understanding of Montessori principles, particularly for those accustomed to traditional educational models?

- Discuss specific strategies such as comprehensive orientation programs, regular workshops, and the use of virtual communication tools like WeChat. Consider these strategies' potential challenges and benefits in enhancing parental involvement and support for Montessori education.

- What are the key differences in family engagement practices between Montessori schools in the United States and China, and how can schools in both countries learn from each other to improve family-school partnerships?

  - Examine the cultural nuances that influence family engagement, such as the emphasis on academic achievement in China versus the focus on holistic development in the United States. Explore how these differences impact family involvement and discuss potential collaborative strategies that could be adopted to foster better family-school relationships.

- How can early childhood educators effectively address and integrate the various types of diversity (cultural, linguistic, socioeconomic, racial and ethnic, ability, family structure, gender, and religion) to create an inclusive and supportive learning environment for all students?

  - Discuss specific strategies educators can use to recognize and celebrate cultural and linguistic diversity in the classroom.

  - Explore the impact of socioeconomic diversity on educational access and outcomes and how schools can support students from different economic backgrounds.

- Analyze the importance of inclusive practices for children with diverse abilities and how to implement them effectively.

- Reflect on the role of family engagement and how understanding different family structures can enhance the educational experience.

- Consider how gender and religious diversity can be respected and supported in early childhood education.

References

Byrd, C. M. (2016). Does culturally relevant teaching work? An examination from student perspectives. *SAGE Open, 6*(3), 215824401666074. https://doi.org/10.1177/2158244016660744

Debs, M., de Brouwer, J., Murray, A., Lawrence, L., Tyne, M., & Wehl, C. (2023). Global diffusion of Montessori schools: A report from the 2022 global Montessori census. *Journal of Montessori Research, (8)*1–15. https://doi.org/10.17161/jomr.v8i2.18675

Derman-Sparks, L., & Edwards, J. O. (2019). Understanding anti-bias education: Bringing the four core goals to every facet of your curriculum. *Young Children, 74*(5).

Epstein, J. L. (2018). School, family, and community partnerships: Preparing educators and improving schools. Westview Press. https://doi.org/10.4324/9780429494673

Epstein, A. (2015). Montessori early childhood teacher perceptions of family priorities and stressors. *Journal of Montessori Research, 1*(1), 1. https://doi.org/10.17161/jomr.v1i1.4939

Epstein, J. L., Sanders, M. G., Sheldon, S. B., Simon, B. S., Salinas, K. C., Jansorn, N. R., Van Voorhis, F. L., Martin, C. S., Thomas, B. G., Greenfield, M. D., Hutchins, D. J. & Williams, K. J. (2019). *School, family, and community partnerships: Your handbook for action.* Corwin.

Freire, P. (2018). *Teachers as cultural workers: Letters to those who dare teach.* Routledge.

Garbacz, S. A., McIntyre, L. L., & Santiago, R. T. (2016). Family involvement and parent–teacher relationships for students with autism spectrum disorders. *School Psychology Quarterly, 31*(4), 478–490. https://doi.org/10.1037/spq0000157

Goonetilleke, R. (2021). The parent-educator relationship in a Montessori education environment: A focused ethnography [Doctoral Dissertation, Creighton University].

Hammond, Z. (2015). *Culturally responsive teaching and the brain.* Corwin.

Hooks, b. (1994). *Teaching to transgress: Education as the practice of freedom.* Taylor & Francis Ltd.

Henderson, A. T., & Mapp, K. L. (2002). *A new wave of evidence: The impact of school, family, and community connections on student achievement.* National Center for Family & Community Connections with Schools.

Jessen, S. B. (2010). *The parent-centered early school: Highland community school of Milwaukee.* Teachers College Press.

Ladson-Billings, G. (1995). Toward a theory of culturally relevant pedagogy. *American Educational Research Journal, 32*(3), 465–491. https://doi.
org/10.3102/00028312032003465

LaRocque, M., Kleiman, I., & Darling, S. M. (2011). Parental involvement: The missing
link in school achievement. *Preventing School Failure: Alternative Education for Children
and Youth, 55*(3), 115–122. https://doi.org/10.1080/10459880903472876

Li, X., & Chen, Y. (2019). The impact of parental workshops on attitudes towards
Montessori education in Beijing. *Journal of Early Childhood Education Research.*

Lillard, A. S. (2005). Montessori: *The science behind the genius.* Oxford University Press.

Lillard, A. S., & McHugh, V. (2019). Authentic Montessori: The dotteressa's view at
the end of her life part II. *Journal of Montessori Research, 5*(1), 19–34. https://doi.
org/10.17161/jomr.v5i1.9753

Lillard, A. S., Taggart, J., Yonas, D., & Seale, M. N. (2021). An alternative to "no
excuses": Considering Montessori as culturally responsive pedagogy. *Journal of
Negro Education.*

Ling Koh, J. H., & Frick, T. W. (2010). Implementing autonomy support: Insights
from a Montessori classroom. *International Journal of Education, 2*(2). https://doi.
org/10.5296/ije.v2i2.511

Montessori, M. (1967). *The absorbent mind.* Holt, Rinehart, and Winston.

National Association for the Education of Young Children (NAEYC). (2020).
Professional standards and competencies for early childhood educators.
https://www.naeyc.org/sites/default/files/globally-shared/downloads/PDFs/
resources/position-statements/standards_and_competencies_ps.pdf

OECD. (2019). *PISA 2018 results (Volume III): What school life means for students' lives.*
OECD Publishing. https://doi.org/10.1787/acd78851-en

Wang, Y., & Zhao, Y. (2019). A Survey on the Application of WeChat Platform on
Home-school Cooperation. *Advances in Social Science, Education and Humanities
Research, volume 357.* Atlantis Press. https://www.atlantis-press.com/proceedings/
iceess-19/125920659

White, H. (2023, October 16). 6 Ways to Create Identity-Safe Montessori Classrooms.
Montessori Life.

Whitescarver, K., & Cossentino, J. (2008). Montessori and the mainstream: A century
of reform on the margins. *Teachers College Record, 110*(12), 2571–2600.

CHAPTER 9

Unleashing the Potential of Montessori Teacher Education in an Increasingly Diverse Global Classroom

By Vanessa Rigaud, EdD, and Cate Epperson, MAT

The adoption of Montessori pedagogy across the globe exists within a rich tapestry of cultural contexts. The legacy of Montessori teacher education informs a tradition that excels in "hands-on experiential learning, education informed by curiosity, and a value for the interconnectedness of the world, diverse people, and learning" (Ward & Bray, 2023, p. 458). Within teacher education programs, adult learners benefit from prepared guides, a thoughtfully prepared environment, opportunities to collaborate with peers, and opportunities for exploration and hands-on learning. After completing a teacher education program, Montessori guides embark on a global educational landscape eager for their participation.

Worldwide, Montessori education is generating excitement due to Dr. Montessori's philosophy, pedagogy, and curriculum, which provide a uniquely holistic education. Interest in Montessori and demand for Montessori programs for children and adolescents continue to increase. According to the recent 2022 Global Montessori Census study, there are 15,763 Montessori schools around the globe, marking a 57% increase in the last 23 years. The "countries with the largest number of Montessori schools were the United States, China, Thailand, Germany, Canada, and Tanzania; the United States, Thailand, the Netherlands, and India have the largest number of government-funded or public Montessori programs" (Debs et al., 2022, p. 7).

In the past decade, significant efforts have been made to integrate diversity and cultural awareness into curriculum instruction. However, challenges persist in creating a curriculum that fully embraces the world's changing demographics (Rigaud & Googins, 2022). The education crisis is exacerbated by a severe shortage of teachers worldwide and is further impacted by recent disruptions in the U.S. education system's infrastructure and opposing racial politics, such as discriminatory policies and practices (UNESCO, 2024). According to UNESCO, an additional 69 million teachers will be required by 2030 to attain universal basic education (2024). This teacher shortage has also significantly impacted Montessori public schools (Newman, 2022).

Current research underscores the need for cultural transformation to enhance learning among our diverse student population in the 21st century (Rigaud & Googins, 2022). Researchers aspire to provide strategies, discourse, and leadership in educational practices that engage all learners for global partnership. Advancing beyond the cultural status quo in classrooms worldwide requires culturally responsive practices and transformation among Montessori educators (Rigaud & Googins, 2022)—including designing multicultural curricula that address various aspects such as race, ethnicity, class, sexual identity, gender, language, nationality, learning differences, religion, and age. This chapter will provide insight into how Montessori teacher education programs can rise to the challenge of preparing teachers for this diverse world.

A Global Community of Montessori Teachers

As of June 2024, 114 teacher education programs were affiliated with the American Montessori Society (AMS). Out of these, 80 were U.S.-based, and 34 were international. These programs offered 245 course levels (177 in the U.S. and 68 internationally). To become a Montessori guide, adults must earn a Montessori teaching credential and, in some cases, an additional state or government teaching licensure. Montessori teacher education programs are generally 1–3 years in duration and are available at different levels, including Infant & Toddler, Early Childhood,

Elementary, and Adolescent. Whether the course is an intensive study course and how much the program implements content beyond the minimum AMS standards can also affect an adult learner's journey.

Montessori teacher education programs can be in-person or partially online (hybrid), and year-round, or during a summer intensive. They can be freestanding or university-based, but most are freestanding (Ackerman, 2019). To obtain a full teaching credential from these programs, adult learners are typically required to have completed a prior bachelor's or master's degree program.

Montessori teacher education programs can sometimes struggle with program infrastructure, financial backing, access to experienced teacher educators, and manufactured curricular materials, especially in the Global South (Debs, 2023). Freestanding Montessori teacher education programs traditionally relying on a low-tech lecture-based model can need more infrastructure and agility to shift course delivery online while maintaining high fidelity and pedagogical integrity. Although Maria Montessori embraced the technology of her time (Park & Murray, 2023), she was deeply committed to the hands-on learning approach embedded in her method and providing a holistic curriculum that focused on the interdependence of humankind and the universe.

In the United States, there are currently over 3.8 million employed teachers. Fifty-one percent of K–12 teachers in both public and private schools have completed their master's degree. Approximately 75% of teachers are women. Regarding racial demographics—as of 2022, the National Center for Education Statistics estimated that 60.9% of the U.S. population identified as white alone, and 57.7% identified as non-Hispanic white. In 2023, the Hispanic population comprised 19.5% of the U.S. population. In 2022, 47.9 million people in the United States identified as Black or African American, making up 14.4% of the total population. (NCES, 2023). The lack of diversity within the education workforce could hinder students and faculty from connecting across differences. However, addressing this issue may lead to the potential positive outcomes of learning in diverse, integrated settings, where the benefits of such an environment can be fully realized as classrooms become increasingly diverse (UCLA Council on Diversity and Inclusion,

2014). While programs face the challenges of attracting and retaining diverse teachers, Montessori teacher education programs can change this trajectory.

Montessori Teacher Preparation through the Lens of Culturally Relevant Pedagogy

Recent research has revealed effective strategies for culturally relevant pedagogy (CRP—also known as culturally responsive pedagogy) and global awareness in the 21st-century classroom. Montessori education benefits significantly from an emerging and innovative approach that deliberately focuses on and delves deeper into multicultural education, an idea Dr. Maria Montessori initially designed with this intention in mind. CRP emphasizes three pillars: 1) academic success, 2) cultural competence, and 3) sociopolitical consciousness. Through CRP, educators can foster an environment that is aware and sensitive to cultural differences, leading to improved academic success, increased engagement in the content, better attendance, and a stronger self-perception of capable learners, particularly students of color. We have seen CRP explored in the previous two chapters in various contexts: here, we will discuss what it looks like for teacher educators to incorporate the pillars of CRP into their teacher education curricula.

What is academic success in Montessori education? Like Dr. Montessori, pedagogical theorist Gloria Ladson-Billings did not focus on academic success as measured by standardized testing; instead, she viewed the whole child, considering their physical, social, emotional, and intellectual abilities. Her work and lectures emphasized students' inner abilities and development. Therefore, according to Ladson-Billings, academic education should be seen as an opportunity for all students to learn and grow (2021, pp. 32–43).

All adult learners in a teacher education program should have access to Montessori materials and pedagogy. In recent years, at our particular institutions, one at a university program and one at a freestanding program, we have deliberately implemented this strategy by focusing on how we deliver Montessori course content. Traditionally, Montessori teacher education has involved long lectures and presentations. However, as adult learners expressed dissatisfaction with this teaching style, we found ourselves at a crossroads. We carefully observed the adult learners and conducted extensive research on content delivery in higher education. The recurring theme that emerged was engagement. As a result, we aimed to find ways to engage adult learners in their academic success. We experimented with various approaches

What is academic success in Montessori education? Like Dr. Montessori, pedagogical theorist Gloria Ladson-Billings did not focus on academic success as measured by standardized testing; instead, she viewed the whole child, considering their physical, social, emotional, and intellectual abilities.

until we settled on a format consisting of 4-hour blocks, comprising 1–2 hours of lecture/presentation and 2 hours of intensive work with the Montessori didactic materials, simulating a child's experience in the classroom. Each adult learner received assignments tailored to their needs and was given 2 hours to complete them. The instructor moved around the room, observing the adult learners and occasionally offering guidance and support when needed. As a result of this approach, we found that adult learners were engaged, enthusiastic, and motivated throughout the work cycle.

Cultural competence is challenging and complex because it involves creating an environment where the community feels a sense of belonging. This includes learners utilizing their backgrounds, languages, histories, customs, and experiences to develop fluency and ease in at least one other culture (Will & Najarro, 2022). Cultural competence, a skill that demands learners to have a firm grasp of their own culture and be proficient in at least one other culture, is not just a choice but a necessity (Ladson-Billings, 2021).

It is crucial to emphasize that all learners, including those who identify as white, must develop cultural competence. In today's diverse, multicultural world, it's beneficial and essential that learners comprehend and appreciate cultures different from their own (Ladson-Billings, 2021). Our teacher education programs engaged adult learners in various ways after we developed a deep sense of diversity, equity, inclusion, access, and belonging. We asked profound and challenging questions about content, perspectives, and perceptions, which led to discussions about culture, inequalities, privilege, and how to challenge existing power structures. As

It is crucial to emphasize that all learners, including those who identify as white, must develop cultural competence. In today's diverse, multicultural world, it's beneficial and essential that learners comprehend and appreciate cultures different from their own. a result, adult learners better understood the curriculum and its relevance to their experiences; they could utilize culture to enhance their grasp of context (Ladson-Billings, 2021).

Sociopolitical or critical consciousness brings relevance to what students learn. Having students—whether they are adult learners or children—make the connection to current events in their lives makes their learning meaningful. Thus, instructors must move beyond lectures and telling to teaching(Ladson-Billings, 2021). Teachers must become skilled in using authentic discussion and debate strategies, cooperative grouping, and small group activities. Additionally, students need access to sliding glass doors to enter other worlds (Ladson-Billings, 2021).

In our Montessori teacher education programs, we also examined the approaches to the curriculum to see our biases toward a Eurocentric lens—a perspective that focuses on European culture and history to the exclusion of other cultures—when presenting the materials. (See Chapter 3 for more discussion on this from the viewpoint of the Montessori classroom guide.) Were we selecting a European flag or puzzle map as a sample when presenting political geography? Were we avoiding difficult conversations because we feared a tense discussion among the adult learners? How were we connecting the content areas of the Montessori curriculum to real-life experiences? Were students just completing valueless checklists, or were they creating valuable work for the community to share their knowledge and concerns via a poster on the library bulletin board, podcasts on the school website, or brochure at the local coffee shop? After examining these and many more thoughts/questions, we adopted new practices in our teacher education programs that would allow adult learners to experience these vital points and essential components of sociopolitical or critical consciousness strategies throughout their coursework.

The Montessori educational approach is timeless and has proven to meet the needs of global society today with its deliberate and precise methodology. Dr. Montessori's scientific and educational work has created a pedagogy that can be adapted to various teaching contexts (Kramer, 1976). Examining a teacher education program through the three pillars—academic success, cultural competence, and sociopolitical consciousness—ensures we stay true to the foundation of the Montessori educational philosophy while intentionally instilling CRP.

Montessori Teacher Education: Global Agency

In the ever-changing landscape of our Montessori classroom environments, the task ahead requires that teachers are ready to integrate CRP with Montessori pedagogy to ensure children and adolescents have all the tools and support they need to succeed. We can anticipate the need for educators to provide children with the skills and knowledge necessary to prepare the next generation for the challenges that await them in this global community. This requires educators to have a range of tools and skills in culturally responsive pedagogy, global awareness, and the ability to appreciate the diversity of culture each child brings into the classroom. By leveraging these tools, educators can create a positive learning environment that supports academic growth and the development of cultural awareness, mutual respect, and peaceful interaction among students from all backgrounds.

To enhance the culturally relevant pedagogy (CRP) in Montessori teacher education programs, program directors and instructors can focus on Ladson-Billings' pillars of academic success, cultural competence, and sociopolitical consciousness. Further research on diversity, equity, inclusion, access, and belonging in Montessori teacher education programs can provide valuable guidance for the next generation of Montessori teachers. It is essential to develop a new generation of Montessori teacher education that embraces the legacy and tradition of Montessori while also looking ahead. To achieve this, teacher preparation institutions must update their programs to meet the demands of 21st-century global schools. As Ladson-Billings (2021) pointed out, "Learning to do a hard reset is not a simple task. It challenges educators to engage and interrogate their own worldviews and develop the facility to move from the center to the margins" (p. 77).

Discussion Questions

- What aspects of Ladson-Billings' three pillars of academic achievement/student learning, cultural competence, and sociopolitical/critical consciousness are embedded in your teacher education program?

- What aspects of the three pillars might you need to incorporate? How might you do this?

- What demographic shifts have you noticed in your adult learner population? How could you increase outreach to various populations to increase diversity among adult learners?

References

Ackerman, D. J. (2019). *The Montessori preschool landscape in the United States: History, programmatic inputs, availability, and effects*. Educational Testing Service. Retrieved https://www.montessoripublic.org/wp-content/uploads/2019/04/Ackerman-2019-ETS_Research_Report_Series.pdf

Debs, M., de Brouwer, J., Murray, A. K., Lawrence, L., Tyne, M., & von der Wehl, C. (2022). Global diffusion of Montessori schools: A report from the 2022 global Montessori census. *Journal of Montessori Research, 8*(2), 1–15. https://doi.org/10.17161/jomr.v8i2.18675

Debs, M. (2023). Introduction: Global Montessori education. In A. Murray, E.T. Alhquist, M.

McKenna, M. Debs (Eds.), *The Bloomsbury handbook of Montessori education*. Bloomsbury Academic.

Kramer, R. (1976). Maria Montessori: A biography. Putnam.

Ladson-Billings, G. (2021). Critical race theory—What it is not! *Handbook of critical race theory in education*, 32–43. https://doi.org/10.4324/9781351032223-5

National Center for Education Statistics. (2023). Characteristics of Public School Teachers. Condition of Education. U.S. Department of Education, Institute of Education Sciences. Retrieved https://nces.ed.gov/programs/coe/indicator/clr.

Newman, S. (2022). Teacher education under attack. *Journal of Education for Teaching, 48*(1), 1–6. https://doi.org/10.1080/02607476.2021.2014241

Park, E. K., & Murray, A. K. (2023). Montessori education in the digital age. In A. Murray,

E.T. Alhquist, M. McKenna, M. Debs (Eds.), *The Bloomsbury handbook of Montessori education*. Bloomsbury Academic.

Rigaud, V. M., & Googins, J. (2022). Disrupting institutional racism in higher education. In Bender-Slack, D. A. & Godwyll, F. (Eds.), *Towards anti-racist educational research: Radical moments and movements* (pp. 103–122). Rowman & Littlefield.

UCLA Council on Diversity and Inclusion. (2014). *Diversity in the Classroom*. https://diversity.ucla.edu/about-codi/ucla-council-on-diversity-and-inclusion-codi

United Nations Educational, Scientific and Cultural Organization–UNESCO (22 February 2024). *Global report on teachers: What you need to know*. https://unes.co/adw69d

Ward, G. C., & Bray, P. M. (2023). Interdependent impact: Contemporary teacher education and Montessori teacher preparation. *The Bloomsbury Handbook of Montessori Education*, p. 457.

Will, M. & Najarro, I. (April 18, 2022). What is culturally responsive teaching? *Education* Week. https://www.edweek.org/teaching-learning/culturally-responsive-teaching-culturally-responsive-pedagogy/2022/04

CHAPTER 10

Advancing Access to Montessori Education through Advocacy

By Heather Gerker, MEd, Vyju Kadambi, MEd, Denise Monnier,
and Wendy Shenk-Evans, MDiv

Imagine a teacher (a product of public Montessori education herself) launches her career at a public Montessori school after completing her master's degree in education and obtaining a Montessori credential. However, the state teacher licensure system doesn't acknowledge Montessori credentials, requiring her to complete an additional 33 credit hours of traditional teacher preparation coursework within 2 years at a personal cost of $5000. Because these requirements often deter Montessori teachers in the United States from entering the public school system, she finds herself the sole Montessori-trained teacher across four classrooms at her level. She must rotate through all classrooms to provide lessons to students.

During her busy first years in the classroom, this same teacher prepares to testify before the state legislature, advocating for a pathway to a state teaching license for Montessori-credentialed teachers. Her story captivates legislators, shedding light on the policy gaps that affect educators like her. Eventually, the legislation passes, but only after the teacher has fulfilled the additional state requirements. She now sees herself as an advocate who has catalyzed policy change to create a smoother path for future Montessori teachers and improve public Montessori education in her state. While this is a fictional story, it is a common example of how Montessori teachers can (and do) take several extra steps to ensure they can fully implement Montessori education in both public and private school settings.

Montessori education is a holistic approach to learning that includes several core components working in concert to support a child's education and development (MPPI, 2015b). Turner (1992) describes the Montessori paradigm as a "system...for it includes all facets of a dynamic whole; and when the parts of the Montessori system are working well, the whole becomes more than their sum—a synergy" (p. 19). However, public policy at all levels of government often forces teachers to alter "parts of the Montessori system," compromising, rather than elevating, the fidelity of Montessori classrooms (Block, 2015; Gerker, 2023). Policy barriers not only affect the quality of a Montessori classroom but also impact equitable access to Montessori education, which has been demonstrated to improve student outcomes of academic achievement, social understanding, and executive functions (Lillard et al., 2017).

The advocacy efforts of Montessori educators are paramount to mitigating the potential adverse policy effects on classroom quality and securing equitable access for all children to the numerous advantages offered in Montessori classrooms. Just as Montessori teachers meticulously prepare their classroom environments, it is equally imperative that the Montessori community collaborate to prepare a policy environment in which fidelity to the Montessori approach is honored (Shenk-Evans, 2019). As Hara and Good (2023) state, "Policy is too important and teachers' expertise too great to overlook [other] meaningful ways teachers can be policy advocates at the school, district, state, and national levels" (p. 1).

The Montessori Public Policy Initiative (MPPI) are experts on Montessori policy and advocacy, working to support the Montessori community in creating an effective advocacy voice for quality Montessori education. MPPI began in 2013 when the American Montessori Society (AMS) and the Association Montessori International (AMI/USA) recognized the need to coordinate public policy efforts. As the policy arm of both AMS and AMI/USA, MPPI has supported the formation and success of Montessori advocacy coalitions in over 40 states. The authors of this paper all represent the work of MPPI; Heather Gerker is the MPPI board vice president, Vyju Kadambi is the MPPI advocacy associate, Denise Monnier is the MPPI director of advocacy, and Wendy Shenk-Evans is the former executive director of MPPI.

We contend that when Montessori educators can speak "policy language" to engage policymakers, external policies are more likely to be aligned with Montessori education. As such, in this chapter, we will explore the importance of policy advocacy for Montessori education. First, we offer definitions for the terms we use. Next, recognizing that public policy and equity are intricately integrated, we situate policy challenges and advocacy through an equity lens. Then, we explain current policy barriers and challenges while sharing success stories of Montessori educators as policy advocates across the United States. Our intent is to support current and future Montessori education advocates with a strong foundation of knowledge and action steps to move forward.

Definitions

We offer the following definitions for key terms central to this chapter. These definitions serve as the foundational framework for exploring the ideas presented. By establishing a shared understanding of these key terms, we aim to enable readers to engage with the content in a nuanced and meaningful way.

- *Public policy* is policy made on behalf of the public, but it also pertains to all institutions, both public and private. Public policy related to education can encompass laws, regulations, and funding priorities created by a government entity (MPPI, 2015a).

- *Advocacy*, as defined by the Alliance for Justice, is any action that speaks in favor of, recommends, argues for a cause, supports or defends, or pleads on behalf of others. According to their Definitions and Examples document, some activities that could be advocacy work are organizing, educating legislators, educating the community on issues, and providing advocacy training, research, and regulatory efforts (AFJ, 2008).

- *Policy advocacy* is specific advocacy conducted to create or change public policy.

- *Policymakers* include anyone in a position to create a policy, rule, or regulation. The term *policymaker* may refer to federal or state legislators, district leadership such as board members or administration, employees of various regulatory agencies such as departments of education, offices of early childhood, and more.

- *Montessori Essentials:* published by the Montessori Public Policy Initiative, delineate the core elements of a Montessori classroom in terms of curriculum, teacher credential requirements, environment, and assessments (MPPI, 2015b). The elements defined in *Montessori Essentials* support Montessori educators in using a unified voice to speak with policymakers.

Equity in Policy

Education policy, primarily generated at the state level, is complex. Several state agencies and departments often oversee the numerous policy areas that impact both public and private Montessori schools. In addition to these state-level policies, public school teachers must navigate district-level policies. Just as public schools must adhere to additional regulations, private schools must also adhere to additional regulations if they receive money from federal and/or state funding streams such as universal preschool or childcare subsidies. Because education policy is created with conventional models of education in mind, principals and leaders of Montessori schools must hold the often-untenable dual accountability—to the Montessori Method and to policies imposed by federal, state, and district-level policymakers (Borgman, 2021).

Increasingly, access to high-quality early childhood and K–12 education while promoting progress toward racial equity is of utmost importance to many policymakers (Katz & Acquah, 2023). As states reckon with both historic and ongoing education inequities, policymakers must use an equity lens to examine and rectify systemic biases that harm BIPOC (Black, Indigenous, and People of Color) families, families in lower income brackets, and other marginalized groups. By definition, equity requires individualization. The Annie E. Casey Foundation (2023) describes equity as recognizing "the shortcomings of [a] 'one-size-fits-all' approach" and understanding "that different levels of support must be provided to achieve fairness in outcomes" (para. 2). Unfortunately, public policy is often created without the kind of nuance that equity demands.

Policies within childcare regulations or public school districts can constrict the implementation of the Montessori approach, compromising the fidelity of the Montessori method and, therefore, reducing Montessori program quality and outcomes. However, Montessori educators are not alone in experiencing challenges with education policies that may shape their teaching pedagogy. For example, Indigenous language reclamation schools dedicated to revitalizing Native languages frequently face challenges such as English language testing requirements, which compromise their core mission (Chew & Tennell, 2023), or they self-exclude from early-childhood funding programs like Head Start, which require testing for English language proficiency using tests given in English. Policies with an equity lens could resolve this issue by funding children to attend language reclamation programs while preserving Native language instruction. Policies could support all children—no matter what type of school they attend.

Another example of a challenge education policy created comes from Illinois, where policymakers mandated a significant number of health and safety trainings for all early childhood providers, giving the providers 5 months to complete them to retain their childcare license (Burke, 2018). While many trainings were available online, several were only offered in English. Providers experienced many barriers to this training policy, including language barriers, internet access, transportation issues, and the potential for lost income if their program had to close so they could attend the training sessions. Consequently, many family childcare providers could not complete the trainings in time and had to close. Programs that closed were predominantly in the lowest socioeconomic neighborhoods, which already tend to have the fewest number of options for childcare (Burke, 2018).

There are numerous reasons that policy may be created without an equity lens. Policymakers are stretched thin or may not have the ability or knowledge to forecast who is inadvertently harmed or left out when drafting policies. They may fail to consult a robust enough group of community members in the process. And this is why the voice of advocates is so crucial. Advocates must inform the policy process to shape policy with the breadth needed to create equitable educational opportunities. Hara and Good (2017) explain,

> It is imperative that researchers, policymakers, and stakeholders carefully consider and get messy in the specifics of policy. It is in the details, the individual contexts, and the lived realities of particular educational policies that we are able to understand their importance and their capacity to elicit real change. (p. 433)

Policy Challenges and Advocacy Success

An advocate is a person who gives voice to a need or issue in order to change policy. While anyone can be an advocate, it is certainly helpful to first understand current policy barriers and challenges (Davis et al., 2020). This section explains policies that may shape the implementation of Montessori education. First, we describe two key areas where policy challenges are common: 1) early childhood and 2) public school systems. Then, we share policy challenges and success stories that span across the private and public sectors.

Early Childhood

Spurred by the federal Office of Early Childhood's Race to the Top Early Learning Challenge in 2011, which mandated the implementation of a Quality Rating Improvement System (QRIS, a system that assesses the level of quality in childcare or preschool and is aligned to traditional education pedagogies), most states shifted to enhance the quality of their early childhood programs. Early childhood experts assert that teacher qualifications, group size, adult-child ratios, curriculum design, and assessment methods are key factors that influence program quality (Chaudry et al., 2017). As such, states have introduced, revised, and expanded various programs and policies related to these identified factors to ensure every child has access to high-quality early childhood education.

Programs and policies that have been introduced or expanded include:

- Childcare licensing regulations
- Funding streams such as childcare subsidies and universal preschool programs
- Quality Rating Improvement Systems
- Workforce Registries (a career lattice used to evaluate teacher qualifications, placing teachers at different levels depending on their credentials)

Further, state funding used by public preschool programs often combines several funding streams, including Head Start, Child Care assistance subsidy, and the blending of public and private dollars (Friedman-Krauss et al., 2020; Wallen & Hubbard, 2013). Many states are moving toward creating "mixed delivery systems," in which early childhood services are supported through public dollars and offered in various settings, including homes, centers, schools, and community-based organizations. Developing these mixed delivery systems across the country acknowledges that policymakers and legislators may actually understand that one size does not fit all for children and families.

Unfortunately, early childhood Montessori programs face challenges because much of the research that informs early childhood policy is predominantly conducted in traditional, often single-age classrooms with teacher-led approaches. Advocates and policymakers then extrapolate, assuming that research would be equally applicable in every context.

Public School Systems

The Montessori Method is one of the most prominent alternative approaches to education and continues to grow as a school choice in the American public school system (Borgman, 2021; Brown, 2015; Debs, 2021; Murray & Peyton, 2008). There are approximately over 600 public Montessori schools in the United States currently (NCMPS, n.d.). The push for Montessori in public schools began in the late 1960s when, in response to the civil rights movement, Montessori education gained support from large urban school districts. For example, in 1967, Roslyn Williams founded CHAMP (the Central Harlem Association of Montessori Parents) to integrate Montessori preschools in New York. Williams believed that Montessori education should not be the "rich child's right"; instead, it should be the "poor child's opportunity" (Debs, 2018). However, many challenges over the years limited the growth of Montessori education in public schools, particularly challenges related to policies that inhibit the ability to implement high-fidelity Montessori education, such as curricula regulations, class size, mixed-age groupings, and teacher licensure (Block, 2015; Borgman, 2021; Brown, 2015; Fleming et al., 2023; Gerker, 2023; Murray & Peyton, 2008). Despite these hurdles in integrating the Montessori model, Montessori schools hold promise within the public sector (Fleming et al., 2023). At the same time, the difficulties that Montessori programs in public settings experience as they strive to fully adopt the Montessori approach pose significant equity issues (see Chapter 4). Children from economically disadvantaged families should not receive a Montessori education that differs from the educational experience of their peers in private Montessori schools.

Policy Challenges and Success Stories
Across Private and Public Sectors

Private and charter schools tend to have more autonomy granted by their independent status. Public schools, however, are bound by accountability measures. This dichotomy reflects the multifaceted challenges and opportunities across the private and public educational landscapes. At the same time, several policy challenges span both sectors.

Approved Curricula

Challenge: States aim to guarantee that children receive education through a high-quality curriculum, with several incorporating Montessori or other research-based curricula into their approved options. Yet, many states do not currently recognize Montessori education as an "approved curriculum" at the early childhood level. Inclusion of the Montessori curriculum is of utmost importance, particularly in states where childcare subsidy payments may be linked to QRIS ratings that are contingent on using an approved curriculum. In addition, universal pre-K (UPK) and other public funding sources often require participating providers to select an approved curriculum. Recognizing that Montessori's comprehensive approach aligns with or surpasses state criteria for curriculum opens up opportunities for families relying on public funding to enroll their children (MPPI & Build Initiative, 2023).

Success story: Not long ago, Montessori schools in Florida abruptly discovered that Montessori was absent from the list of approved curricula to be chosen by providers in the state's universal preschool program. This lapse in approval left these schools with a stark choice: either adopt a different curriculum or turn away families who relied on UPK funding. A quick survey of preschool programs revealed that at least 50 schools and over 500 children would be impacted. Montessori advocates rolled their sleeves up to tackle the bureaucratic maze. Through a well-coordinated effort, they successfully petitioned for a waiver for the year and the opportunity to submit their curriculum for approval. United in purpose, Montessori educators in Florida, alongside the Montessori Public Policy Initiative (MPPI), acted swiftly. Through their collective efforts,

Montessori education, once again, found its place on the approved list of curricula, rescuing not just the schools but ensuring the continuity of the Montessori approach for the enrolled families.

Ratios, Group Sizes, and Mixed-Age Groups

Challenge: A Montessori classroom includes several essential pedagogical components. Among them, higher ratios, group sizes, and 3-year mixed-age groupings are crucial. Because they are integral to the Montessori approach, larger class sizes, higher ratios, and mixed-age groups are also core components of Montessori school accreditation standards (MPPI & Build Initiative, 2023). Yet most licensing requirements call for smaller ratios, group sizes, and single-age groups.

Success story: In an early policy triumph, Maryland collaborated with its education department to secure special permission within childcare regulations for Montessori schools to operate with higher ratios and group sizes. Fast-forward several years, and the state unveiled a universal preschool program, complete with legislation mandating a 1:10 adult-child ratio and a cap of 20 students per classroom. A well-intentioned move designed to increase quality threatened to disqualify public and private Montessori schools from enrolling families reliant on UPK funding. Enter a team of local Montessori advocates, who educated legislators about the Montessori approach and aligned themselves with the state's goal of giving all children access to high-quality early learning environments. They then leveraged the existing policy allowances for group sizes and ratios within childcare regulations and were successful in getting an amendment to the UPK legislation passed. This amendment ensured that public and private Montessori schools retained the flexibility to maintain their unique educational model while serving children through the universal preschool program.

Montessori Credential Recognition

Challenge: There are currently 11 colleges and universities with AMS Montessori teacher preparation embedded in either bachelor's or master's degree programs, indicating the academic rigor of Montessori teacher education (AMS, n.d.). However, because most Montessori teacher preparation programs are at freestanding institutions, as opposed to connected to institutes of higher education, many states are unaware of the depth and breadth of knowledge that Montessori credential holders possess. As such, Montessori credentials often do not qualify an individual for a state teaching license, universal preschool lead teacher status, or advanced placement in other state systems. Eleven states currently have a pathway for individuals with a bachelor's degree and a Montessori credential to obtain a teaching license. In the remaining states, public schools must hire state-licensed teachers and then send them to a Montessori teacher education program for Montessori credentialing. With most Montessori teacher education programs taking place across multiple years, it is possible for a student not to have a fully trained teacher for the entirety of their 3-year cycle at a given level, thus compromising the fidelity of Montessori education offered in that classroom. In addition, schools have to pull funds from other budget areas to pay for their non-Montessori teachers to attend a Montessori teacher education program.

Success story (in process): In some cases, alternative solutions to legislation may be necessary. At least 10 states currently have a policy pathway for Montessori teachers to obtain state licensure. In one state, experienced and dedicated advocates, with the support of MPPI, have been working on teacher licensure bills. After considerable time and effort, the first bill died when the sponsoring legislator left the committee before it could be heard or discussed during an election year. Montessori advocates worked to connect with a new legislator whose children attend a Montessori school. This new legislator and their staff have spent considerable time exploring the landscape to see how the bill will be received and what opposition will be—anticipating concerns from the state Department of Education and teacher unions. The state's teacher licensing system is complex, with many alternate routes. Advocates have met with multiple representatives of alternate pathway programs (different approved paths for teachers to obtain a state teaching license) and reviewed comparisons of the various program requirements and those of Montessori credentials. This analysis has led the advocates to conclude that pursuing one of these alternative routes would result in additional and duplicative work, additional time, and significant financial costs for teachers. These conclusions and concerns were shared with the Department of Education and the legislative staff regarding whether one of the alternate route programs is to be used as a pass-through for Montessori credentialed educators. Advocates have become articulate on the legislative process, the state licensure requirements and pathways, the alternative route pathways, and how each affects Montessori teachers, schools, and students. This state is an excellent example of the number of twists and turns that can be involved in policy change and the importance of learning from and adding that experience to the advocacy toolbox as the work moves forward. An agreement has not yet been reached, but the dedication and persistence of the advocates assure that it will be the best possible option when a pathway is put in place.

Support for Current and Future Montessori Advocates

"Montessori was also a practical activist who recognized that it was important to translate her beliefs into practical methods" (Loeffler, 1992, p. xvi). Following in Dr. Montessori's footsteps, Montessori educators must learn how to shift from using Montessori terms for the pedagogy's tenets and principles to a language understood by others—particularly to a language understood by policymakers. Recent research shows that external policy mandates are the most common barriers to authentic Montessori implementation in schools, which shapes educators' ability to implement authentic Montessori in many ways (Borgman, 2022; Culclasure et al., 2018; Gerker, 2023). We contend that when Montessori educators can speak the "policy language" and policymakers listen, external policies may align more with Montessori education.

We must also remember that we cannot "learn to be an advocate by just reading about it or talking about it" (Davis et al., 2020, p. 17). Educators need to be informed. Educators need to know how to take action and feel supported in doing so. Supporting educators in understanding how to use their voices in the policymaking process can be accomplished in many ways. First, teacher education programs should introduce Montessori teachers to education policy and provide opportunities to engage in policy processes (Gerker, 2023; Jones et al., 2017). Second, public school districts and boards of private schools should encourage teachers to engage in policy through professional learning communities (Jones et al., 2017). Finally, school leaders can support Montessori teachers by listening to their experiences and expertise and including them in decision-making (Gerker, 2023). These suggestions perhaps make the issue at hand seem simplistic when, in reality, systemic forces create barriers for teachers, such as inadequate teacher planning time or unsupportive administrators, that prevent them from engaging in advocacy or the policy-making process (Good, 2019). The work of MPPI and other advocates continues to push against policy barriers, nudging teachers to become more involved in advocacy and encouraging systems surrounding teachers to be more supportive.

But how do we get policymakers to listen? As shared previously, there are many success stories of Montessori advocates across the country who have united to be informed about policy and to speak out in efforts to shape policy decisions. In an ideal world, legislators invite teachers to participate in policymaking (Davis et al., 2020). Until then, Montessori educators must unite to make their voices heard and advocate for developing educational policies that better align with and address Montessori education's specific needs and principles.

We have seen the strength of Montessori policy advocates in action! Recently, Montessori-credentialed teachers have moved into policymaking positions in their state, teachers are initiating and participating in conversations with district leaders and state officials, and more advocates are reaching out to MPPI to learn more about the *Montessori Essentials* (personal communication with the MPPI team). Montessori parents have also led and collaborated on legislative advocacy campaigns, some teacher education programs now include advocacy in their coursework, and more state officials who have chosen Montessori for their own children are acknowledging the need for broad access to Montessori and open to policy change to create that access.

As our advocacy work to support policy change for Montessori education expands, connections and collaborations become even more important. Speaking with a unified Montessori voice, connecting that voice through our existing system of state advocacy organizations, and working for inclusive policies using broadly defined parameters like the MPPI *Montessori Essentials* is the pathway to a future where Montessori education is accessible by all.

Interested in getting involved? Visit https://montessoriadvocacy.org/ to find your state advocacy group, access resources and tools for advocacy, and sign up for the MPPI newsletter.

Discussion Questions

- We are all Montessori advocates in our own ways. What does advocacy look like for you? How might you elevate your advocacy efforts to increase access to Montessori education?

- What does "speaking with a unified voice" mean to you? How might this support you in your advocacy for Montessori education?

- How might you become active in your state's advocacy organization? If there isn't a group, how might you start one?

References

Alliance for Justice (AFJ). (2008). *What is advocacy?*
https://mffh.org/wp-content/uploads/2016/04/AFJ_what-is-advocacy.pdf

American Montessori Society (AMS). (n.d.). Find a teacher education program.
https://amshq.org/Educators/Montessori-Careers/Become-a-Montessori-Educator/
About-AMS-TEP/Find-A-TEP

Annie E. Casey Foundation. (2023). *What's the difference between equity and equality?*
https://www.aecf.org/blog/equity-vs-equality

Block, C. R. (2015). Examining a public Montessori school's response to the pressures
of high-stakes accountability. *Journal of Montessori Research, 1*(1), 42–54.
https://doi.org/10.17161/jomr.v1i1.4913

Borgman, C. (2021). *Enacting accountability in innovative schools: The sensemaking
strategies of public Montessori principals* [Doctoral dissertation, University of Virginia].
Archive, University of Virginia. https://libraetd.lib.virginia.edu/public_view/
w95051224

Brown, K. (2015). *Montessori programs in urban public schools: Policy and possibilities*
[EDCI Policy Brief]. Urban Education Collaborative.
https://public-montessori.org/wp-content/uploads/2016/10/Montessori-Programs-
in-Urban-Schools-Policy-and-Possibilities-Katie-Brown.pdf

Burke, C. W. (2018). 90 days until no paycheck: Time running out for Illinois childcare providers in subsidy program. Chalkbeat Chicago. https://www.chalkbeat.org/
chicago/2018/10/10/21105907/90-days-until-no-paycheck-time-running-out-for-illi-
nois-child-care-providers-in-subsidy-program/

Chew, K. A. B., & Tennell, C. (2023). Sustaining and revitalizing Indigenous languages
in Oklahoma public schools: educational sovereignty in language policy and planning.
Current Issues in Language Planning, 24(1), 60–80. https://doi.org/10.1080/1466420
8.2022.2037289

Chaudry, A., & Morrissey, Taryn & Weiland, C. & Yoshikawa, Hirokazu. (2017).
Cradle to kindergarten: A new plan to combat inequality. Russell Sage Foundation.

Culclasure, B., Fleming, D. J., & Riga, G. (2018). *An evaluation of Montessori education
in South Carolina's public schools.* The Riley Institute at Furman University.
https://www.furman.edu/wp-content/uploads/sites/195/rileypdfFiles/
MontessoriOverallResultsFINAL.pdf

Davis, J. M., Ethridge, E., & Beisly, A. H. (2020). *Empowered educators: Lessons gleaned
from the Oklahoma walkout.* In Advocacy in Education (Ed. Ethridge, E. et al)

Debs, M. (2018). *Jeff Bezos and the trap of the charitable-industrial complex.* The New York Times. https://www.nytimes.com/2018/09/23/opinion/jeff-bezos-pre-schools-montessori.html

Debs, M. (2021). *Diverse families, desirable schools: Public Montessori in the era of school-choice.* Harvard Education Press.

Fleming, D. J., Culclasure, B. T., Warren, H., & Riga, G. (2023). The challenges and opportunities of implementing Montessori education in the public sector. *Journal of Montessori Research & Education, 4*(1). http://10.16993/jmre.19

Friedman-Krauss, A. H., Barnett, W. S., Garver, K. A., Hodges, K. S., Weisenfeld, G. G., & Gardiner, B. A. (2020). *The state of preschool 2019: State preschool yearbook.* National Institute for Early Education Research.

Gerker, H. E. (2023). Making sense of Montessori teacher identity, Montessori peda-gogy, and educational policies in public schools. *Journal of Montessori Research, 9*(1).

Good, A. G. (2019). *Teachers at the table: Voice, agency, and advocacy in educational policymaking.* Lexington Books.

Hara, M., & Good, A. G. (2023). *Teachers as policy advocates: Strategies for collaboration and change.* Teachers College Press.

Hara, M., & Good, A. G. (2017). Introduction: Teacher voices in and on educational policy. *Peabody Journal of Education, 92*(4), 433–434.

Jones, D., Khalil, D., & Dixon, R. D. (2017). Teacher-advocates respond to ESSA: "Support the good parts—Resist the bad parts." *Peabody Journal of Education, 92*(4), 445–465.

Lillard, A. S., Heise, M. J., Richey, E. M., Tong, X., Hart, A., & Bray, P. M. (2017). Montessori preschool elevates and equalizes child outcomes: A longitudinal study. *Frontiers in Psychology, 8.* https://doi.org/10.3389/fpsyg.2017.01783

Loeffler, M. H. (Ed.). (1992). *Montessori in contemporary American culture.* Heinemann Educational Books.

Katz, H. T., & Acquah, E. O. (2023). Tackling racial equity in US schools: A critical policy analysis of enacted state legislation (2020-2022). *Journal for Critical Education Policy Studies* (JCEPS), 21(1).

Montessori Public Policy Initiative (MPPI). (2015a). What is public policy? https://montessoriadvocacy.org/wp-content/uploads/2024/01/What-is-Public-Policy-2-6-2019.pdf

Montessori Public Policy Initiative (MPPI). (2015b). Montessori Essentials. https://montessoriadvocacy.org/wp-content/uploads/2019/07/MontessoriEssentials.pdf

Montessori Public Policy Initiative (MPPI) & Build Initiative. (2023). *Broadening policy for mixed delivery: Incorporating Montessori programs in state quality improvement systems.* https://montessoriadvocacy.org/wp-content/uploads/2023/01/MPPI-QIS-report-1-23-23.pdf-FINAL.pdf

Murray, A., & Peyton, V. (2008). Public Montessori elementary schools. *Montessori Life, 20*(4), 26.

National Center for Montessori in the Public Sector (NCMPS). (n.d). About the Montessori census. https://www.montessoricensus.org/about-the-montessori-census/

Shenk-Evans, W. (2019). Montessori advocacy: Preparing the public policy environment. *Association Montessori International USA Journal,* Spring, 20–22.

Turner, J. (1992). Montessori's writings versus Montessori practices. In M. Loeffler (Ed.), *Montessori in contemporary American culture* (pp. 17–47). Heinemann Educational Books.

Wallen, M., & Hubbard, A. (2013). *Blending and braiding early childhood program funding streams toolkit.* Ounce of Prevention.

CHAPTER 11

Montessori and Adult Development: Theory to Practice

By Katie Keller Wood, EdD

Through the education and development of children and adolescents, Montessori education has long been seen as a vehicle for creating a more peaceful and just world. However, the Montessori approach also has important implications and applications for adult development. Dr. Montessori wrote on adult development vis-a-vis the transformation of the teacher, as well as in her writings to parents. Yet, to move Dr. Montessori's vision for a better world forward, the Montessori community of today has much to offer adults both inside and outside our Montessori school communities. This chapter aims to show that utilizing Montessori approaches in adult education has the potential to not only support adult learning and skill development but also to support holistic adult development, thereby increasing the capacity of adults to work and live with greater joy, self-confidence, and purpose in an ever-changing world. In the same way that Montessori classrooms aim to support the normalization and valorization of children and adolescents, a Montessori approach can support the self-actualization of adults, equipping them to navigate the adaptive challenges of our increasingly complex world.

This chapter is organized into three sections. Section one seeks to establish a Montessori approach as a best practice not only for children, but also for adults, by comparing Montessori methods to the leading theory of adult learning. Section two discusses leading theories of adult development to show how the overarching goals of Montessori education have much in common with the "highest" forms of human development. This discussion is important both to place the Montessori community in greater conversation with leading scholarship regarding adult development, and to make the case for Montessori as a viable option for promoting holistic adult development. Finally, section three builds on the arguments and research of the first two sections to examine the practical applications of a Montessori approach for adults. Three areas of application are examined: 1) Montessori teacher education and professional development, 2) workforce development (reskilling/upskilling) for adults more generally, and most broadly of all, 3) a discussion of how applying a Montessori approach to work and life might support the kind of holistic adult development required for the creation of a more peaceful, just, equitable, and sustainable world.

Montessori: Pedagogy or Andragogy?

The best-known theory of adult learning in the United States is that of Malcolm Knowles, who was not the first to coin the term *andragogy* but whose theory of andragogy became the most widely known. Knowles created this theory under the supposition that adults have different learning needs than children, and if *pedagogy* (from the Greek *paidos*, meaning "boy or child" was the word to describe education for children, *andragogy* (from the Greek root *Andr-*, "adult male") was the best term for the education of adults.

Jarvis (1985, p. 51) charts a comparison between pedagogy and andragogy, according to Knowles' theory, noting that within a pedagogical framework, Knowles assumed that:

- Students are dependent learners, unable to be self-directed.

- Students do not have significant experiences to draw from, so teaching methods must be didactic (the "empty vessel" approach).

- Others decide what knowledge is important (not the student), so a standardized curriculum is utilized.

- Learning is oriented around acquiring the subject matter at hand, so curriculum is organized into subject disciplines.

This is contrasted with an andragogical approach, where Knowles posited that:

- Learners are independent and self-directed, so the role of the teacher shifts to supporting the student's self-directed learning.

- Learners have significant life experiences, which can serve as a resource for learning. This allows a shift from lecture-style teaching to incorporating problem-solving and discussion-based learning activities.

- Students are intrinsically motivated to learn, so learning programs are oriented around real-life application and relevance.

- Learning experiences should be based on issues or problems to be solved, as opposed to general topics or content, so their utility is clear.

Comparing these two contrasting lists, Montessorians will quickly recognize that the Montessori approach has much more in common with Knowles' perspective on andragogy, not pedagogy.

Yet Knowles' theories do have several limitations. One of these, relevant here, is that Knowles' theory presupposes a pedagogy based on a classical curriculum framework, whereas a romantic curriculum (Lawton, 1973) is another option. As described by Jarvis (1985), these two frameworks often contradict one another. He wrote:

"Education from above" assumes a classical curriculum form whereas "education of equals" reflects a romantic curriculum. In the former, the emphasis is on the social system and the individual is prepared to fit into it; education is a kind of initiation into society, rather than an extension of socialization: in the latter, the emphasis is placed upon the individual and his ability to achieve his potential so that he can act as an agent in society. (p. 49–50)

Jarvis posits that while Knowles' views of pedagogy assume a classical curriculum framework, andragogy refers to a more romantic curriculum framework (p. 51). The Montessori approach, with its emphasis on intrinsic motivation, child/adolescent self-construction, and teacher as a guide, would certainly fall under the romantic curriculum approach as well.

Summary

Knowles's theory of andragogy, the most common theory regarding best practices of adult education, has much more in common with a Montessori approach to education than the conventional "pedagogy" of his theorizing. It stands to reason, then, that many of the best practices for (especially older) Montessori students may also provide rich developmental learning environments for adults. Indeed, Montessori teacher education programs and professional development opportunities (two areas of adult learning within the Montessori community) are at their most robust when they also model best practices of the Montessori classroom. These practical applications are the topic of section three.

Adult Development Theory

There are a variety of theories related to adult development, and a Montessori perspective can fit well with many of these. While Montessori's Method was not focused on adult development per se, there are nevertheless significant overlaps between the goals of Montessori education (described by Montessori as both normalization and valorization) and adult development theory. In addition, Montessori herself was not silent on the development of adults. While most of her writings on adult development are focused on the transformation of the teacher, she also addresses parents and other adults. Jendza (2023) describes that while "the Montessori approach is oriented to the child" (and adolescent), "Montessori was also very clear about the role of adults in education" (p. 167).

Lawrence Kohlberg

Lawrence Kohlberg was an American psychologist whose work focused on exploring moral and ethical development, proposing a stage-based model that has several commonalities with other models of development. Carol Gilligan adapted Kohlberg's model, proposing slightly different stages for women, and arguing that men and women think differently about morality (1977). Gilligan's model also had limitations, including an emphasis on the gender binary, and neither model included a cross-cultural perspective. More recent scholars on moral development (e.g., Gibbs et al., 2007) have looked more closely at the role of culture as an important factor for developing moral choices and behavior.

Nevertheless, some elements of Kohlberg's theorizing have found utility for Montessori scholars. Jendza (2023) utilizes Kohlberg's work as "an intriguing interpretive frame in which the adult Montessori practitioners and their (trans) formation can be characterized for a better understanding of the holistic nature of Montessori education" (pp. 167–168). Analyzing how Montessori teachers might move through Kohlberg's preconventional, conventional, and postconventional stages of development, from relying on external authority figures (like trainers) to drive their work to working to achieve social acceptance in their schools and workplaces to internalizing a set of personal norms which allows for the questioning of conventions and becoming critical agents of Montessori practices, Jendza argues that the transformation of a Montessori teacher may move teachers beyond "a process of routine adult formation" (p. 169). Jendza's point is an important one: if the Montessori community is going to continue to evolve and impact the world, we need critical practitioners dedicated to peace and justice as described in Chapter 7. This requires adult development.

Jane Loevinger

Jane Loevinger was an American developmental psychologist who offered a developmental theory for ego development through the lifespan. As described by Manners and Durkin (2001), Loevinger saw the ego as "a holistic construct representing the fundamental structural unity of personality organization" (p. 542).

Throughout the lifespan, Loevinger posited that humans moved through the nine sequential stages as they developed increasing capacities and skills across four domains of development (Manners & Durkin, 2001). Loevinger ascribed the first four stages to children and adolescents, with the later stages occurring in late adolescence and adulthood. The final stage, called *integrated*, is most closely associated with Maslow's concept of self-actualization, where the person "is growth motivated, seeking to actualize potential capacities, to understand [their] intrinsic nature, and to achieve integration and synergy with the self" (Manners & Durkin, 2001, p. 544).

This is an important point, as Montessori practitioners will see commonalities in the goals of Montessori education and Loevinger's "integration" and Maslow's "self-actualization." Maslow described self-actualizing individuals as "people who have developed or are developing to the full stature of which they are capable" (1954, p. 201). He also wrote that "Self-actualizing people are... involved in a cause outside their own skin, in something outside of themselves... something which fate has called them to somehow and which they work at and which they love, so that the work-joy dichotomy there disappears" (Maslow, p. 110). There are many similarities with Maslow's self-actualization and Montessori's concepts of "cosmic task" and the role that work plays in connecting a human to the cosmos.

In addition, Rathunde (2015) suggested that, based on Montessori's writings about teacher preparation, it may be that "a key component of teacher preparation for Montessori education is self-actualization" because "in Maslow's terms, such a person would be ... better able to promote another's self-actualization" (p. 20). Thus, for students and adults, Montessori's goals have much in common with Maslow's self-actualization.

Robert Kegan and Eleanor Drago-Severson

Robert Kegan's constructive-developmental theory (1982, 1994) is one of the most widely used theories of adult development. Eleanor Drago-Severson grounds her work on adult development on this theory as well. Like Kohlberg and Loevinger, Kegan provides a stage-based framework for adult development. As described by Drago-Severson (2008), Kegan's "constructive-developmental theory ... centers on two fundamental premises: a) We actively make sense of our experiences (constructivism); and b) The ways we make meaning of our experiences can change—grow more complex—over time (developmentalism)" (p. 61).

Drago-Severson describes the stages of Kegan's theory as "ways of knowing" (2009, chapter 1, "Acknowledging Developmental Diversity," para. 5). She wrote that the most complex stage "is becoming increasingly prevalent in postmodern society" (2009, chapter 2, "Ways of Knowing," para. 1). Drago-Severson and Kegan both ascribe the increasing rates of adults at this highest stage to the increasing complexity of the world, where adaptive challenges, for which "solutions lie outside the current way of operating" (Heifetz, 2010, p. 73) are more common, and so greater human development is required.

In further describing adults with this highest "way of knowing," Drago-Severson (2009) states that:

> [They] have grown into the developmental capacity to take perspective on their own authorship, identity, and ideology, forming a meta-awareness.... Self-transforming knowers have the capacity to examine issues from multiple points of view and... [are] also able to understand and manage tremendous amounts of complexity (chapter 2, "The Self-Transforming Way of Knowing," para. 7).

In addition, Drago-Severson notes that "adults with this way of knowing understand that one's own perspective is incomplete and that one's self is also incomplete without intimate relationships with others" (2009, chapter 2, "The Self-Transforming Way of Knowing," para. 9).

Like Montessori's emphasis on the teacher's transformation, both Kegan and Drago-Severson posit that there is a difference between informational learning and transformational learning and that only the latter can move a person to greater developmental capacities, equipping them for a world of increasing complexity.

Summary

While all theories of adult development have limitations, there are striking commonalities between the goals of Montessori education and the "higher" stages of development as described by several of the most prominent adult development theorists. The experiences required for such adult development also have commonalities with Montessori's most discussed theme related to adult development: the transformation of the teacher. Thus, applying Montessori's theories and methods to adult development, and not just to the education of children, may provide an important vehicle for supporting a more fully actualized, interconnected, and growth-oriented adult who can manage the increasing complexities of our world. In this way, a Montessori approach to adult education, just like the approach for the education of children and adolescents, may prove a vehicle for creating a more peaceful and just world.

Applications of Montessori for Adult Development

This final section of the chapter builds on the arguments and research of the first two sections to examine practical applications of a Montessori approach for adults. Three areas of application are examined: 1) Montessori teacher education and professional development, 2) workforce development for adults more generally, and finally, 3) an even broader discussion of how a Montessori approach might support capacity-building for any adult.

Montessori Teacher Education and Professional Development

While Montessori was chiefly concerned with the education of children, there was one category of adult development that received significant attention in her writings: the transformation of the teacher.

Cossentino (2009) described Montessori teacher education as a unique paradigm. She wrote that:

> For Montessori, the prepared adult was a central means of revolutionizing education. The teacher is meant to serve as the embodiment of a new vision of education as an aid to life. To achieve this goal, Montessori teacher preparation aims directly toward transforming the adult's attitudes toward learning and human relationships. (p. 525)

She continued, "The preparation of the adult entails a fully integrated conception of the adult as guide. The practice of Montessori education ... is directed toward the moral and spiritual goal of fulfilling human potential" (Cossentino, 2009, p. 525–526).

Montessori teacher education and professional development are at their most robust when adults are not only taught the principles and skills required for Montessori education but when they also have the chance to have Montessori principles and practices modeled for them in an experiential way.

Montessori teacher education and professional development are at their most robust when adults are not only taught the principles and skills required for Montessori education but when they also have the chance to have Montessori principles and practices modeled for them in an experiential way.

Thus, in the same way that Montessori classrooms consider the holistic needs of the children and adolescents that they serve, Montessori teacher education programs must also support adult learners as whole people. This requires a shift away from the top-down, classical curricular framework still common in some settings. It will mean that teacher education programs build in time to gather regular feedback on pacing, support, and self-assessed learning and progress. Trainers must remember that learning, along with the spiritual preparation of the teacher, doesn't always occur in a linear fashion. Adult learners need opportunities to engage and re-engage with important content, much like children experiencing Montessori's spiral curriculum, to gain deep understanding. If long days of in-person training are utilized, adult learners need opportunities for community-building, uninterrupted work and processing time, movement, reflection, and even playtime, just as a Montessori classroom would provide. That said, there's no reason that online coursework can't also take these human needs into account, with assignments for taking some quiet reflection time, opportunities for community engagement, and more. Teaching and assessment methods must also be considered: extensive lecturing, high-stakes assessments, and a lack of differentiation would not be present in a high-quality Montessori classroom, so such methods for adults must also be replaced by increased opportunities for direct practice, guide and peer feedback, discussion, and reflection. Assignments and assessments must provide differentiated options, allowing adult learners choices that meet their needs and allow them to show learning in a variety of ways. And faculty must work with adult learners to co-create Montessori learning environments that center equity and belonging for all. In the same vein, professional development must be similarly responsive to the needs of adult learners. Please see Chapter 9 for further discussion regarding best practices for Montessori professional development.

Of course, Montessori teacher education is not immune to challenges, including a lack of diversity among instructors, ensuring culturally affirming and anti-bias learning materials and experiences, and modeling best practices for inclusion, to name a few. A 2023 dissertation study by Bass-Barlow regarding BIPOC (Black, Indigenous, and People of Color) teachers' experiences of training programs indicated some significant needs in this area. As the director of a Montessori teacher education program myself, I think Bass-Barlow's work contains important insights for all Montessori teacher educators. Yet, compared with more conventional approaches for adult learning and development, which are often lecture-based and lack differentiated supports for learners, the best practices of Montessori teacher education, as outlined above, may provide a viable model for other adult learning and development.

Montessori Applications to Workforce Development

Younes (2023) proposed that the Montessori Method might serve as a guiding framework for adult education, particularly when it comes to workforce development and the reskilling and upskilling diverse groups will need for an ever-changing world. Her thesis reviewed Montessori applications to adult learning and recommended guiding principles for utilizing a Montessori approach for adult workforce development. Specifically, Younes proposed that adult learning programs demonstrate respect for individual experiences and human potential, offer opportunities for learning through the senses and at one's own pace, provide a prepared environment (as applied to both physical and virtual learning spaces) that takes the holistic needs of adults into consideration, offer opportunities to foster independence and autonomy within (and while contributing to) a vibrant learning community, and provide learning opportunities and materials that allow for self-correction and self-direction. Such principles show the adaptability of the Montessori Method and the potential for applications beyond Montessori schools and training programs.

Younes also reviewed the Montessori Method for Orienting and Motivating Adults (MOMA) project (Boldrini, 2015). This project, supported and funded by the European Commission, developed a framework for adult education grounded in Montessori principles. The MOMA project consisted of several educational projects taking place in several different European countries, which were all designed to serve adults viewed as being at risk of marginalization in an "effort to overturn the traditional assumptions determining strong barriers to the involvement of vulnerable target groups in the formal educative systems" (Part 1, page 1). The groups varied greatly in age, gender, and background, and group descriptions were not uniform, so some information was limited. Nevertheless, the MOMA project described the following participants:

- A group of adults in Italy who were identified as being not in education, employment, or training, who were also characterized as having living situations characterized by social isolation. This group participated in the MOMA project via an English-language learning course.

- A group of adults in the UK who were identified as being immigrants who had experienced difficulty accessing traditional adult learning in the UK due to cultural and language barriers. This group participated in the MOMA project via a series of workshops.

- A group of migrant women from Russia and Ukraine in Germany at different stages of learning German, who were unemployed and trying to find employment. This group participated in the MOMA project via vocational workshops.

- Roma adults in Lithuania, who were identified as being part of one of the most marginalized groups in Europe (facing high levels of discrimination), and who participated in the MOMA project via fishing workshops.

- Senior adults (all over age 50, and with an average age of 64) in Portugal, who participated in the MOMA project via either Spanish language classes or classes on Cognition and Aging.

Montessori principles utilized in the MOMA project included the absorbent mind, learning environment, experimentation and exploration, observation, and independence. Each of these principles was further clarified to show how that principle would manifest in the program. For example, the principle of absorbent mind was explicated to convey an emphasis on personalization and co-creation of the learning experiences, an emphasis on community, intellectual stimulation and critical thinking, and diverse teaching methods designed to meet a variety of learner needs.

In applying these principles to several different groups engaging in various adult learning experiences across Europe, the MOMA project reported that the application of Montessori principles to these experimental learning groups was successful, with testimonials related to participant engagement and empowerment, but also indicated that more study was needed to effectively report on outcomes (Younes, 2023). Unfortunately, it is difficult to find additional information on this project beyond the published MOMA manual, and the website momaproject.eu is no longer functional.

Montessori Applications to Adult Development

Finally, my current work (e.g., TEDx Talks, 2023) considers additional applications of the Montessori approach for adult development (the kind of self-actualization and development described by adult development researchers as being increasingly necessary in our world of increasing complexity) particularly regarding how adults might think about the intersection of their own work and lives. Montessori's ideas of work offer some counter cultural perspectives to modern society's (often conflicting) messages about the appropriate role of work in modern adult life, especially when considering Montessori's cosmic approach. Indeed, Montessori classrooms are known for incorporating meaningful work, providing opportunities for uninterrupted work, allowing choice based on interest, blurring the lines between work and play, and valuing all types of work. Students learn that their unique skills and assets are needed in the classroom community (and, by extension, in the world) and that everyone has an important role. In addition, Montessori classrooms take a holistic approach to child development, ensuring that students are supported in their academic, social, emotional, physical, and even spiritual development. I maintain that robust adult development, the kind of developmental experiences that can lead to transformational learning and better equip adults to live and work in a world of increasing complexity, requires a similar holistic approach.

Summary and Conclusion

Montessori approaches for adult development, including teacher education, professional and workforce development, and broader adult development, are not well-tested. Still, there is a strong theoretical backing and some encouraging preliminary research to show that utilizing a Montessori framework may also aid in adult development and learning. If so, it seems likely that adult education, just like the education of children and adolescents, may also prove an important vehicle for fulfilling Montessori's vision for a more peaceful and just world.

Discussion Questions

- How might you apply Montessori philosophies to your own adult development or your work with other adults?

- How might reflecting on adult learning theories support your pedagogical practice?

References

Bass-Barlow, K. (2023). *Examination of Montessori training: Experiences of people of color inpublic and charter Montessori* schools [Doctoral dissertation (Ed.D.), Arkansas StateUniversity]. https://www.proquest.com/docview/2856660597

Boldrini, F. (2015). Montessori Method for orienting and motivating adults: Guide for the application of the Montessori Method to adult education. MOMA.

Drago-Severson, E. (2008). Pillars for adult learning. *Journal of Staff Development, 29*(4), 60– 63.

Drago-Severson, E. (2009). Leading adult learning: Supporting adult development in our schools. SAGE Publications. Kindle Edition.

Cossentino, J. (2009). Culture, craft, & coherence: The unexpected vitality of Montessori teacher training. *Journal of Teacher Education, 60*(5), 520–527.

Gibbs, J. C., Basinger, K. S., Grime, R. L., & Snarey, J. R. (2007). Moral judgment development across cultures: Revisiting Kohlberg's universality claims. *Developmental Review, 27*(4), 443–500.

Gilligan, C. (1977). In a different voice: Women's conceptions of self and of morality. *Harvard Educational Review, 47*(4), 481–517.

Heifetz, R. A. (2010). Adaptive work. *The Journal Kansas Leadership Center*, spring, 72–77.

Jarvis, P. (1985). *The sociology of adult & continuing education.* Routledge.

Jendza, J. (2023). Adult formation to transformation. In A. Murray, M. Debs, M. McKenna & E.

M. T. Ahlquist (Eds). *The Bloomsbury handbook of Montessori education.* (pp.167–174). Bloomsbury Academic.

Kegan, R. (1982). *The evolving self: Problems and process in human development.* Harvard University.

Kegan, R. (1994). *In over our heads: The mental demands of modern life.* Harvard University.

Lawton, D. (1973). *Social change, educational theory and curriculum planning.* University of London Press.

Manners, J., & Durkin, K. (2001). A critical review of the validity of ego development theory and its measurement. *Journal of Personality Assessment, 77*(3), 541–567.

Maslow, A. H. (1954). *Motivation & personality.* Harper & Row.

Rathunde, K. (2015). Creating a context for flow: The importance of personal insight and experience. *NAMTA Journal, 40*(3), 15–27.

TEDx Talks. (2023, September 29). *Work-life balance is a lie: Finding alignment* | Kathryn *Keller Wood* [Video]. YouTube. https://www.youtube.com/watch?v=_LM1yS3TzTk

Younes, R. (2023). *A Montessori approach to workforce development and future-ready adult learning.* Master's Thesis, OCAD University. https://openresearch.ocadu.ca/id/eprint/3968/1/Younes_Rania_2023_MDES_SFI_MRP.1.pdf

CHAPTER 12

Paving the Path to a Transformative Future

By Munir Shivji, MEd and Gina Taliaferro Lofquist, MEd

This book has explored various facets of Montessori philosophy and practice and the Method's application across different spheres of life. From the foundational principles established by Dr. Maria Montessori to the innovative strides taken by the American Montessori Society (AMS), from the unique pedagogical approaches in Montessori classrooms to the integration of technology, sustainability, and social justice, the previous chapters have navigated the intricate tapestry that defines Montessori education in contemporary culture.

Collectively, these topics illustrate the dynamic and transformative potential of Montessori education. In this concluding chapter, we weave these themes into a cohesive vision for the future, reflecting on current trends, challenges, and the potential for transformative change on a global scale. The potential for Montessori education to enact positive change has never been greater; Montessori's transformative power can extend beyond individual classrooms, shaping entire communities and societies.

> The potential for Montessori education to enact positive change has never been greater; Montessori's transformative power can extend beyond individual classrooms, shaping entire communities and societies.

We will outline a forward-looking roadmap for Montessori education, inspired by the strategic behind-the-scenes work of AMS, that will evolve our practices to meet the challenges and opportunities of the 21st century.

In this chapter, we explore high-level issues and considerations that affect Montessori education. We briefly discuss each issue and then offer ideas and strategies for where to go in the future. These ideas and strategies are meant to be starting points. We acknowledge that each Montessori community is unique and that you will adapt these ideas to fit your community's specific needs and aspirations. Choose strategies that resonate with your vision, set reasonable, actionable goals, and work to bring them to fruition. By doing so, you will contribute to the continuous evolution of Montessori education and help shape a future where its benefits are accessible to all. We invite you to embrace what lies ahead with optimism and creativity, continuing to transform lives through the power of Montessori education.[10]

Supporting Montessori Teachers and Adult Learners

Montessori education is at a crossroads, facing both unprecedented opportunities and challenges. As the interest in Montessori expands globally, there is an urgent need for credentialed professionals who can uphold and advance the Method's principles and practices. Complicating this are the various cultural needs and the lack of experienced educators to support growth in regions where Montessori is still emerging. Additionally, the changing dynamics of work-life balance and shifting generational expectations call for innovative approaches to teacher preparation and retention.

Adding to these challenges is the national decline in the current generation pursuing the teaching profession: In 2021–2021, postsecondary institutions granted more than two million bachelor's degrees, a 146% increase from the numbers recorded 50 years ago. However, while education was once the most popular field for a bachelor's degree, making up one-fifth of all conferred degrees in 1970–1971, it has dropped drastically over the years. In 2000–2001,

---

10 As employees of AMS, Executive Director (Munir) and Senior Director of Education and Strategic Initiatives (Gina), we hold a unique perspective on the Montessori community and its evolving landscape. However, we want to clarify that the ideas and suggestions presented in this chapter are our own and do not necessarily reflect the official views or positions of AMS.

just 8% of degrees were in education; by 2021, this dropped to 4% (LaMonte & Torres, 2024). This decline underscores the urgent need for innovative strategies to attract and retain educators in the Montessori field—a more specialized sector within the broader educational landscape.

Montessori educators are the driving force behind the transformative power of Montessori education. Becoming a Montessori teacher is a journey that requires time, dedication, critical thinking, reflection, and a deep understanding of Montessori philosophy beyond the use of materials. The transformation of the adult is a central tenet of teacher preparation, calling for self-awareness, self-reflection, character development, and care of one's emotional health. It encourages an internal audit of one's biases, openness to differences, and respect for the potential of *all* children.

In our complex, ever-changing world, it is essential that we engage adult learners to better meet their needs while also preserving the integrity of the transformational process and of Montessori education. Innovation in teacher preparation is both necessary and possible to provide opportunities for self-transformation through intentional high-quality training, even when using varied teaching modes.

As we face a global shortage of teachers and a lack of accessibility to high-quality Montessori teacher education, blended learning models can enhance inclusivity and diversity while mitigating the current impact of this shortage. By combining traditional in-person training with online components, we make teacher preparation more accessible without diluting the essence of Montessori education. Now is the time to implement changes to broaden the reach of a deeper pool of qualified Montessori teachers. Montessori schools and teacher education programs can establish partnerships to recruit and educate new teachers.

Once new teachers join the Montessori field, retaining them is vital for maintaining continuity and stability. Again, schools and teacher education programs must collaborate to create supportive environments that encourage continuous professional growth. Here are some more strategies and specifics:

Montessori Values in Online Learning: Developing flexible and accessible pathways for Montessori teacher education will help meet the growing demand for qualified educators while creating supportive environments that encourage long-term commitment and professional growth, which will ensure the stability and quality of Montessori education. Teacher education programs can:

- Create a rich blended curriculum that integrates online modules and in-person learning experiences.

- Utilize learning management systems like Canvas to deliver online courses.

- Design online content and online interactions that embody Montessori values, such as self-directed learning, individualized pacing, and learner choice.

- Establish online forums, study groups, and peer mentorship networks where adult learners can collaborate, share experiences, and support each other's learning journeys.

- Enhance engagement with multimedia resources such as video tutorials, podcasts, interviews, virtual simulations of Montessori environments, and readings.

- Implement ongoing assessment strategies that combine online quizzes, self-reflection, peer reviews, and in-person evaluations.

Online platforms provide comprehensive student performance, engagement, and interaction data, including discussion participation, assignment submissions, quiz analytics, grades, and detailed activity logs. This data, observations, and intentional reviews of submitted content can help educators track progress, identify at-risk students, and enhance learning experiences. It also guides the much-needed regular, constructive feedback that helps adult learners progressively develop their skills and understanding (Race & Brown, 2005). AMS-affiliated teacher education programs can access costly tools like Canvas directly as a benefit of their affiliation.

An Understanding of and Commitment to Innovation: A cohesive and well-informed teacher education program (TEP) team is essential for driving innovation within the program. Innovation must be rooted in a solid grasp of the starting point: an internalized understanding of the TEP's values, ethos, expected learner outcomes (including application of knowledge), and incorporation of Montessori tenets. Collaborative faculty, equipped with a thorough understanding of the TEP and its expected outcomes, can use their assessment of adult learners' experiences to identify gaps and roadblocks and innovate solutions accordingly. This approach facilitates continuous improvement of the learner experience and outcomes, program leadership, and program culture. Investment in faculty development is critical to promoting an atmosphere of innovation. AMS offers two programs, Teacher Education Instructor Academy and Online Onboard, which are focused on equipping educators with the skills and knowledge necessary to deliver programs effectively and foster innovative teaching practices.

Cultural Competency and Inclusivity: Teacher education programs can incorporate training on cultural competency and inclusive teaching practices into their online and in-person components. For example, they can ensure the curriculum reflects diverse perspectives and prepares educators to work in multicultural environments.

Partnerships for Practical Experience: Teacher education programs can develop partnerships with established Montessori schools to provide adult learners with internship opportunities, real-world classroom observations, and access to experienced Montessori educators. These partnerships can also facilitate resource sharing and joint professional development initiatives.

Mentorship Programs: Newly credentialed Montessori teachers can be paired with experienced mentors who can provide guidance, support, and practical advice. These mentors can assist with classroom leadership, lesson planning, and navigating the school culture, which can be particularly beneficial during the initial years of teaching.

Professional Learning Communities: Professional Learning Communities (PLCs) allow Montessori teachers to collaborate regularly to share best practices, discuss challenges, and engage in joint problem-solving. These communities can focus on specific areas such as curriculum development, student assessment, or integrating new technologies into the classroom. In addition, schools can encourage teachers to participate in local and national Montessori networks and conferences and can offer or support memberships in professional organizations and involvement in community outreach programs that align with Montessori values.

Career Growth Pathways: Clear pathways for career growth within the Montessori framework will aid in teacher retention. This might include roles such as lead teacher, curriculum coordinator, or administrative positions. Once these roles have been identified, schools can offer professional development opportunities that align with these career tracks, such as training in leadership or advanced Montessori methods. AMS currently offers the Emerging Leaders Fellowship Program, the Curriculum Coaching Academy, and certificates in advanced studies in reading, writing, and science.

Supportive School Cultures: Schools can foster a culture that values collaboration, open communication, and mutual respect. This includes encouraging and soliciting regular feedback from teachers about their work environment and then using this feedback to make meaningful improvements. Celebrating successes and acknowledging the hard work of staff can go a long way.

Integrating Research and Technology

While Montessori education traditionally limits the use of digital technology, particularly for young children, the reality of our digital world cannot be ignored. Technology use is also a practical life skill and relevant instruction can close the technology gap for socioeconomically disadvantaged students. Montessori principles can be aligned with technological advancements through careful and thoughtful integration that respects the developmental needs of children. Supporting children's development as intelligent and empathetic digital citizens is necessary for both their academic and social lives. Now that digital technology is a significant part of our culture, we have a responsibility to build healthy bridges that help children and adolescents navigate their learning with these tools effectively and responsibly.

Integrating digital and other technology thoughtfully into educational experiences is crucial for enhancing student learning and engagement. Research indicates that when technology is effectively integrated into the curriculum, it can support personalized learning, foster collaboration, and help children develop critical thinking skills. According to the International Society for Technology in Education (ISTE), technology should not just be an add-on. Instead, it should be used to transform learning experiences in meaningful ways (Crompton, 2017). Additionally, studies have shown that technology can help bridge educational gaps, providing access to resources and opportunities for all students, regardless of their background (Pane et al., 2015). By leveraging research-based strategies, Montessori educators can ensure that developmentally appropriate technology enhances the learning process rather than detracting from it, ultimately preparing students for the demands of the 21st-century workforce.

Digital tools can enhance Montessori education without compromising its core principles. For example, digital record-keeping and assessment tools can streamline administrative tasks, allowing teachers more time to focus on direct engagement with students. Additionally, virtual experiences and online resources can extend Montessori learning beyond the physical classroom and traditional one-dimensional paper charts, cards, and visuals, supporting connections with diverse and global communities and real-world experiences.

To thoughtfully integrate digital technology into Montessori education while respecting its core principles and the developmental needs of children, schools, and educators can adopt specific guidelines and strategies that empower Montessori educators to use technology to enhance learning and streamline administrative tasks without detracting from the hands-on, child-centered nature of Montessori classrooms. Here are some ideas:

- **Digital Technology Integration:** Schools and educators can establish clear guidelines for using digital technology in the classroom to ensure it complements, rather than replaces, hands-on learning. Digital literacy concepts can be integrated into the Montessori curriculum to teach students about responsible and ethical use of technology, including lessons on internet safety, respecting online privacy, and understanding digital footprints. To lay the groundwork for all this, educators can participate in training and professional development on effectively integrating digital tools into teaching: seek out workshops on using specific educational technologies, best practices for balancing screen time, and strategies for incorporating digital resources into Montessori lessons.

- **Technology for Enhanced Learning Experiences:** Digital platforms can connect Montessori classrooms with peers worldwide, fostering global awareness and cultural exchange. Programs like Go Pangea (gopangea.org) can facilitate connections, allowing students to collaborate on projects and share their learning experiences with a global audience. Online resources can also provide immersive learning experiences that can complement Montessori lessons. For instance, a lesson on the solar system can be enhanced with virtual tours of space provided by platforms like NASA's Eyes or Google Earth.

- **Evidence-Based Practices and Action Research:** Current research findings on the use of technology in educational environments can help guide how educators adopt technology in Montessori classrooms. A data-driven approach, whether to technology specifically or to Montessori teaching methods and classroom practices more broadly, can help refine, improve, and lend credence to Montessori in today's contemporary context. For instance, strategies can be adopted from recent studies showing how Montessori methods improve student outcomes in math, reading, and social "soft" skills. Action research—in which educators use their classroom data and observations to inform and improve their practice (Mertler, 2021)—can also be particularly useful. This approach aligns with the scientific basis of Montessori education and can provide valuable insights into effective teaching strategies and student outcomes. Schools can encourage Montessori teachers to conduct action research in their classrooms and provide professional development and resources for designing and conducting studies. Before teachers enter the classroom, teacher education programs can incorporate research methodology and findings so adult learners learn to evaluate research critically, apply findings to their practice, and conduct their studies to contribute to the field.

- AMS is committed to supporting action research through programs like the Montessori Action Research Symposium (MARS). MARS brings together Montessori teachers and leaders to advance Montessori education through the study and implementation of practitioner action research projects. It serves as a model for further AMS action research programming and studies to grow the number of teachers and leaders engaging in practitioner action research while also disseminating findings from selected research projects.

- **Publication and Dissemination:** Schools and teacher education programs can encourage educators and action researchers to publish their findings in academic journals, at conferences, and through Montessori organizations or other educational groups. It's also worth considering how various media platforms can make research accessible to a broader audience, including parents, policymakers, and the general public. For example, AMS's *Journal of Montessori Research* publishes peer-reviewed articles on Montessori education and is a key outlet for disseminating research.

Fostering Inclusive and Culturally Relevant Learning Environments

For Montessori education to truly thrive globally, it must reflect and embrace diverse perspectives, cultures, and communities. Creating inclusive learning environments requires a commitment to equity, diversity, and social justice (Au, 2014). Montessori schools and educators should actively engage with their students' cultural contexts, integrating culturally relevant materials and practices into their classrooms. Simply celebrating various holidays and incorporating basic lessons on culture and diversity falls short of fulfilling the work of diversity, equity, inclusion, and belonging (DEIB).

Neuroscience research offers various proven approaches for designing and implementing brain-compatible, culturally responsive instructional strategies beyond surface-level inclusivity (Hammond, 2014). These strategies include creating learning environments that recognize and honor the cultural backgrounds of all students, incorporating teaching methods that leverage the diverse ways in which students learn best, and fostering a sense of belonging and psychological safety. By integrating neuroscience insights with culturally responsive teaching practices, Montessori educators can better engage students, enhance their cognitive development, and support equitable learning outcomes.

The AMS (2022) publication *Equity Examined: How to Design Schools and Teacher Education Programs Where Everyone Thrives* is a free, 385-page downloadable audit tool and series of essays designed to help Montessori schools and teacher education programs measure and understand the current state of DEIB within their organizations—recognize strengths, identify areas for improvement, and gain valuable insights to help prioritize and implement meaningful change. Other strategies for fostering inclusive environments include:

Diversity in Curriculum: Our curricula must go beyond tokenism and incorporate teaching methods and content that connect with students' diverse backgrounds. Teachers can offer stories, materials, and lessons that reflect the various cultures, abilities, disabilities, and gender identities in the classroom, ensuring students see themselves in the curriculum. They can explore the histories, languages, music, art, and other contributions of different cultures in depth rather than simply celebrating certain cultures' holidays. They should strive to avoid stereotypes and include voices from marginalized communities. Books, artwork, and resources that depict a wide range of cultures, races, and perspectives should be available and visible—this may require attempts to decolonize curricula, including projects like exploring the impact of non-Western mathematicians or studying ecological systems from Indigenous perspectives.

Community Engagement and Inclusivity: School policies may need to be reworked to promote diversity, equity, and inclusion at all levels, from student recruitment to staff hiring practices, and should be monitored to ensure the policies are communicated clearly and practiced consistently. Teachers and staff can also build strong relationships with students' families and communities by hosting regular cultural exchange events for families to share their traditions, languages, and stories. Global citizenship can be reinforced by developing relationships with Montessori school communities worldwide and having students share their cultures through stories, letters, and videos.

Professional Development and Ongoing Reflection: Cultural competence doesn't occur due to a single day of training, reading a book, or taking a course. Educators become culturally competent over time by committing to ongoing transformation through education and professional development on cultural competence and unconscious bias (Johnston et al., 2017). Schools can encourage educators to reflect on their cultural assumptions and learn strategies for creating a more inclusive and equitable classroom to empathetically and consistently meet the individual needs of all children. Regular self-assessment and reflection sessions can help both educators and students to discuss DEIB issues and identify areas for improvement. Schools can aid in creating a safe space for these conversations and encouraging ongoing dialogue about equity and inclusion.

Mental Health and Well-Being in Montessori: An important component of DEIB is the focus on care of self. The seeds for this are planted in teacher education and must continue as a central focus at the school level. Incorporating mindfulness practices, providing social-emotional learning opportunities, and ensuring a supportive and nurturing environment can help address the mental health needs of both children and educators. Reducing teacher stress will also support increased retention. In addition, it's ideal to provide teachers with training on recognizing and responding to mental health issues (their own as well as students), and offering them education on trauma-informed practices, mental health first aid, and strategies for supporting students with anxiety or depression. Age-appropriate Social-Emotional Learning (SEL) programs can be embedded into the curriculum to teach emotional regulation, empathy, and conflict resolution. Schools can promote and incorporate activities that support physical and mental health, such as gardening, nature walks, yoga, stretching, or outdoor play. Ideally, students' families can be brought into the fold and involved in mental health education and support initiatives.

Commitment to Sustainability and Environmental Education

Montessori education has had a long-standing commitment to respect the natural environment and recognize the interconnectedness of humans with the responsibility of caring for the Earth. Research indicates that integrating sustainability into the curriculum enhances students' environmental awareness, critical thinking, and problem-solving skills (Tilbury, 2011). Montessori schools that adopt sustainable practices reduce their ecological footprint and serve as role models, fostering a culture of environmental responsibility among students. Global citizenship is further actualized by modeling environmental care and engaging students in classroom and community responsibilities. As global environmental challenges become more pressing, Montessori programs should be equipped to lead in promoting sustainability and ecological stewardship.

Schools and teacher education programs should adopt sustainable practices to reduce environmental impacts and create powerful learning experiences for students of all ages. Incorporating environmental education into the Montessori curriculum and making it part of the community focus will foster generations of eco-conscious learners. Outdoor classrooms, gardening programs, and projects focused on conservation and sustainability will help students develop a deep connection to and respect for the natural world (NAAEE, 2016).

Here are some more specific strategies for incorporating sustainability into Montessori curricula:

Environmental Integration: Teachers can integrate environmental topics across various subjects; for instance, teaching science through the lens of ecosystems and biodiversity, or using math to explore energy consumption and carbon footprints. Teachers can use outdoor spaces for regular class activities to get children outside more often. Outdoor classrooms can be simple, like a circle of logs, or more elaborate, with seating and shelter. These spaces can be used for science lessons, art projects, or quiet reading time, connecting students more closely with nature. Students can also engage with practical environmental efforts in urban settings, such as rooftop or vertical gardens to maximize limited space and incorporate urban agriculture practices to foster a sense of ecological responsibility. Project-based learning opportunities can also focus on local environmental issues such as waste disposal, food management, or air pollution.

Student-Led Initiatives: Student-led green teams or sustainability committees can give children a voice in planning and implementing school-wide sustainability practices. These groups can lead initiatives, monitor progress, and educate their community on environmental issues. Students can also take part in projects that promote conservation and sustainability. This could include local clean-up efforts, tree-planting activities, or campaigns to reduce water usage. Projects can be tied to broader learning goals and community involvement. Students can develop gardens to grow vegetables, herbs, and flowers that serve as living classrooms, teaching students about plant biology, ecosystems, and the food cycle. Students can establish and manage robust school-based recycling and composting programs, and work to reduce single-use plastics by encouraging reusable containers and utensils. A "zero waste" policy where students and staff are encouraged to minimize waste production and find ways to repurpose materials is something to consider. Composting organic waste from a school garden can also demonstrate sustainable practices.

Advocacy and Public Policy for Montessori Education

Expanding access to Montessori education requires robust and targeted advocacy and engagement with public policy officials and influencers. Montessori communities must unite to influence educational policies that support and promote high-fidelity Montessori principles and practice, leveraging the official work of the Montessori Public Policy Initiative (MPPI) and the AMS Regional Action Commission (RAC).

Partnering with MPPI while engaging with policymakers and stakeholders at local, state, and national levels is critical. Using a collective voice, we can create a system conducive to the growth and sustainability of Montessori education that advocates for recognition and support of Montessori credentials, funding for Montessori programs, and policies and curricula that align with Montessori's educational philosophy and high-fidelity pedagogical practice (MPPI, n.d.).

Efforts should focus on integrating Montessori methods into public school systems, making this approach accessible to a broader range of students. Advocacy for funding, training, and policy support is essential to facilitate this integration. Here are some more specifics about getting involved:

Policy and Legislative Participation: The National Association for the Education of Young Children (NAEYC) emphasizes the importance of policy and legislative participation, encouraging educators to stay updated and involved in advocacy efforts to promote positive changes in the education system (NAEYC, n.d.). Staying informed about legislative developments that impact education and actively participating in public comment periods, legislative hearings, and advocacy campaigns is vital for advancing educational quality and equity. Educators and local groups can partner with MPPI (montessori-advocacy.org) to amplify advocacy efforts, including organizing meetings and forums with local and state policymakers to discuss the benefits of Montessori education and advocate for supportive legislation. MPPI is designed to lead the efforts and provide resources, training, and strategic support for all Montessori-related advocacy campaigns.

AMS Regional Action Commission: Regional efforts play an important role in building deeper connections within the Montessori community and advocating for Montessori education at the state and regional levels. The Commission provides a network of passionate Montessori educators to collaborate with AMS and partner with MPPI. This collaborative effort ensures that public policy and advocacy efforts are moved forward in an organized and strategic manner, effectively promoting and supporting Montessori education.

Montessori State Advocacy Groups: Working with other Montessori proponents in your state is critical to successful advocacy. Most education policies are created at the state and local levels, and most states (in the United States) have Montessori advocacy coalitions that you can join and support to get involved. These groups provide valuable information on Montessori teacher credential recognition, child-care licensing regulations and subsidies, the Quality Rating and Improvement System (QRIS), and more. Educators can stay updated on policy changes and participate in advocacy efforts by working with state education departments to include Montessori credentials in teacher certification standards to significantly impact the future of Montessori education. Connecting with state advocacy groups is a great way to get information and contribute to the ongoing development and support of Montessori education locally and regionally.

Ensuring Excellence and Growth in Public Montessori Education: State governments play a crucial role in public education by creating policies that control school budgets, curricula, and standards, as well as providing funding and overseeing education policies through state-established school boards. Additionally, states advocate for the construction of new schools and manage the results of state assessments, which can influence curriculum changes. Charter schools, which are public institutions, are particularly relevant to this discussion. They are funded through a combination of tuition charged to school districts, which is based on enrollment-based funding, and other sources such as federal grants and private donations. This unique funding structure allows charter schools to implement alternative educational approaches, including Montessori methods, within the public school system.

The future growth of public Montessori schools in the United States hinges on a balanced approach that blends state autonomy with the supportive role of the federal government, while adhering to the high-fidelity standards outlined in AMS's school accreditation program. Properly credentialed Montessori teachers are essential to this vision, as they possess the skills and expertise necessary to implement high-fidelity, transformative Montessori education.

Families can also play an essential role in this process, advocating for Montessori programming and actively supporting public district, magnet, or charter schools. Their involvement ensures these programs receive the resources and attention needed to thrive. Integrating Montessori principles into public education can further elevate these efforts, offering a personalized, hands-on, and holistic learning model. For example, in Cincinnati, OH, public Montessori schools educate one out of every six children, supported by a strong and organized system of parent advocacy. Although these schools were initially established through desegregation orders that created magnet schools, the growth of Cincinnati Public Schools' Montessori programs has been primarily driven by parent demand and the efforts of dedicated parent organizations. For example, Pleasant Ridge Montessori was developed as a neighborhood school rather than a magnet school, offering a Montessori education to all children within its attendance boundaries. Additionally, formal bodies such as Local School Decision-Making Committees ensure that community members, parents, and teachers collaborate effectively to maintain the integrity and fidelity of the Montessori approach.

Beyond AMS, organizations such as the National Center for Montessori in the Public Sector (NCMPS) and Public Montessori in Action International (PMAI) collaborate with public Montessori schools and districts to provide guidance to support the successful launch of new schools to fully implement Montessori education. Together, families, educators, and stakeholders can ensure that every child has the opportunity to succeed and flourish.

Deepening Parent and Community Engagement

The Montessori approach extends beyond the classroom, involving parents and the broader community in the educational journey. Deepening parent and community engagement is essential for fostering a supportive and holistic educational environment that benefits students' academic and social development. Research shows that when parents and community members are actively involved in schools, students tend to have higher academic achievement, better attendance, and improved behavior (Henderson & Mapp, 2002). Effective engagement strategies include regular communication, collaborative decision-making, and creating opportunities for parents to participate in school activities. Moreover, schools that build strong relationships with their communities can leverage local resources and expertise to enhance educational programs and provide real-world learning experiences. By prioritizing meaningful parent and community engagement, schools can create a more inclusive and responsive educational system that supports the success of all students.

Community involvement in Montessori education can help spread its benefits and create a more inclusive and connected society. Encouraging parents to join in advocating for Montessori in their communities and states will strengthen efforts for recognition. The parent voice is powerful, and we must consider how to effectively bring them into this work.

Here are some ideas on how to deepen engagement with families and communities:

- **Natural Partnerships:** Montessori philosophy naturally involves partnerships between home and school, child and teacher. Enhancing these partnerships by engaging more deeply with parents, caregivers, and other community members, as well as through open communication, shared goals, and collaborative efforts, can deepen relationships. This supports each child's development and creates an educational ecosystem beyond the classroom.

- **Outreach Programs:** Parents/caregivers and community members can be enlisted in advocacy efforts to promote and expand Montessori education in these ways and others:

  - Create ambassador programs where parents and educators share the benefits of Montessori with other communities, helping to spread its principles and practices.

  - Develop partnerships with local educational institutions to introduce Montessori practices and demonstrate their effectiveness, thereby increasing the Method's reach and impact.

  - Form parent-led committees or groups to organize Montessori-based activities and volunteer efforts, such as organizing a book fair or starting a school garden.

  - Implement outreach programs to bring Montessori education to underserved communities, offering Montessori Early Childhood programs in community centers or partnering with local organizations for parenting classes.

  - Use Montessori methods in various community settings, such as libraries, museums, and after-school programs, to create environments that support self-directed learning and exploration; explore using Montessori approaches in senior centers to support individuals with dementia through activities that promote independence and cognitive engagement.

  - Recruit tech-savvy parents and caregivers to help promote Montessori through social media and other media sources.

Imagining the Future of Montessori Education

As we look to the future, the potential for Montessori education to bring about positive change is immense. By addressing current challenges and embracing opportunities for innovation, Montessori can continue to thrive and expand its influence globally. The core principles of Montessori, deeply rooted in understanding and nurturing the individual child, remain profoundly relevant and transformative as we navigate the complexities of modern education.

As educators, parents, and advocates of Montessori, we hold the power to shape its future. Together, we can expand access to Montessori education, innovate in teacher preparation and retention, and foster environments that celebrate diversity and holistic development. By staying true to Montessori's vision while embracing contemporary advancements, we can ensure that Montessori education thrives, inspiring generations of learners to reach their fullest potential. Together, we can uphold Dr. Maria Montessori's legacy, adapt to society's changing needs, and continue to empower children worldwide with the tools to build a better, more compassionate future.

Discussion Questions

- How can the foundational aspects of Montessori be applied or adapted to contemporary issues in your school or teacher education program?

- What do you think will be the most significant challenges in the future for Montessori education? What will be the most significant opportunities?

- What ideas do you have for how Montessori education can expand around the globe? How can you advocate for this growth and support Montessori education for diverse and underrepresented populations, ensuring equity and inclusion?

References

American Montessori Society (AMS). (2022). *Equity examined: How to design schools and teacher education programs where everyone thrives.* https://www.amshq.org/EquityExamined

Au, W. (2014). *Rethinking multicultural education: Teaching for racial and cultural justice* (2nd ed.). Rethinking Schools.

Crompton, H. (2017). *ISTE standards for educators: A guide for teachers and other professionals.* International Society for Technology in Education.

Hammond, Z. (2014). *Culturally responsive teaching and the brain: Promoting authentic engagement and rigor among culturally and linguistically diverse students.* Corwin.

Henderson, A. T., & Mapp, K. L. (2002). *A new wave of evidence: The impact of school, family, and community connections on student achievement.* National Center for Family & Community Connections with Schools.

Johnston, E., D'Andrea Montalbano, P., & Kirkland, D. E. (2017). *Culturally responsive education: A primer for policy and practice.* Metropolitan Center for Research on Equity and the Transformation of Schools, New York University.

LaMonte, H., & Torres, A. (2024). What's behind the teacher shortage? *National Association of Independent Schools.*

Mertler, C. A. (2021). *Action research: Improving schools and empowering educators* (6th ed.). SAGE Publications.

Montessori Public Policy Initiative (MPPI). (n.d.). Our work. https://montessoriadvocacy.org/our-work/

National Association for the Education of Young Children (NAEYC). (n.d.). Become an advocate. https://www.naeyc.org/get-involved/advocate

North American Association for Environmental Education (NAAEE). (2016). *Early childhood environmental education programs: Guidelines for excellence.* Washington, DC.

Palloff, R. M., & Pratt, K. (2007). *Building online learning communities: Effective strategies for the virtual classroom.* Jossey-Bass.

Pane, J. F., Steiner, E. D., Baird, M. D., & Hamilton, L. S. (2015). *Continued progress: Promising evidence on personalized learning.* RAND Corporation.

Race, P., & Brown, S. (2005). *The online learning handbook: Developing and using web-based learning.* Routledge.

Tilbury, D. (2011). *Education for sustainable development: An expert review of processes and learning.* UNESCO.

ABOUT THE AUTHORS

Dana Anderson, MS, is a children's digital content expert, writer, and Montessori guide. Currently, she teaches Language Arts and Digital Citizenship at Bridgemont International School, a virtual school based in Florida. Dana has worked with tech companies on issues related to high-quality digital content for kids; her writing has appeared in dozens of publications, and she authored *The Complete Idiots' Guide to Vegan Eating for Kids.* Dana is AMS-credentialed at the Primary and Elementary levels and is currently working on her Adolescent credential.

Geoffrey Bishop is the executive director and founder of Nature's Classroom Institute (NCI), an environmental education program serving students from over 100 Montessori schools across the United States. He is also the executive director of a Montessori school on 140 acres in Mukwonago, Wisconsin, blending his expertise in environmental education with the Montessori philosophy, serving students from age 3 through high school. Geoffrey serves on the AMS Board of Directors, is chair of the Global Committee, and sits on the Finance and Executive Committees.

Olivia Christensen, PhD, has worked in education since she was 12. Her roles in the field have included (but are not limited to) babysitter, nanny, summer camp art teacher, Montessori preschool guide, graduate researcher, teacher educator, and early childhood specialist for the Minnesota Department of Education. Liv is passionate about the value of early childhood education and is committed to supporting the field in ways that promote equity and justice.

Genevieve D'Cruz, PhD, is an educator and researcher based in Hyattsville, MD. She is the founder of Lee Montessori Public Charter School in Washington, D.C. Her research focuses on anti-racist teaching to support BIPOC teacher and student identities in the Montessori classroom. She works with Public Montessori in Action International to conduct research to support Montessori schools in the public sector.

Cate Epperson, MAT, is the academic director at Hope Montessori Educational Institute, an AMS-affiliated Montessori teacher education program in St. Louis, MO. She is a doctoral student at Webster University researching transformative learning in Montessori teacher education programs. Cate serves as a Teacher Education Action Commission commissioner for the American Montessori Society.

Heather Gerker, MEd, is a PhD candidate at the University of Cincinnati, where she is focused on policy research that shapes the Montessori pedagogy. She has spent more than a decade working in Montessori education as a researcher, a teacher, a teacher educator, and a teacher education program director. Heather is an educational researcher at the University of Kansas, serves on the AMS Research Committee, and is vice president of the Montessori Public Policy Initiative board.

Sarah Hassebroek, EdS, is a former instructional coach, literacy coach, and Elementary Montessori teacher. She is an associate professor at St. Catherine University in Saint Paul, MN, teaching graduate and undergraduate programs. She is also a consultant and workshop presenter on literacy and instructional leadership topics.

Seth Johnson, MS, is an Upper Elementary teacher at Lexington Montessori School in Lexington, MA. He is a Montessori Elementary Teacher Training Collaborative faculty member and completed the American Montessori Society Emerging Leaders Fellowship in 2020. Seth has presented at local and national Montessori conferences on ecological sustainability, self-regulation, autonomy, and systems thinking. He is AMS-credentialed (Elementary I–II).

Allison Jones, MEd is a Primary- and Elementary-trained Montessorian with 20 years of experience, including teaching, coaching, special education, school administration, bilingual Montessori, and DEI in school settings. She holds an MEd from Loyola University. Her passion is ensuring that Montessori is implemented in a way that serves all children and is rooted in each child's identity and community.

Vyju Kadambi, MEd, is the state advocacy associate with the Montessori Public Policy Initiative (MPPI). In her nearly 25 years as a Montessori educator, she has served as a teacher, head of school, and school founder. She has worked in both private and public Montessori schools and strongly believes that there needs to be greater access to high-quality Montessori education for all families.

Katie Keller Wood, EdD, is the Executive Director of CMStep: the Cincinnati Montessori Secondary Teacher Education Program. She is also an adjunct instructor for the MEd program at Xavier University and the EdD program at the University of Wisconsin-River Falls. Since 2016, Katie has supported and engaged in Montessori research through the Montessori Research Working Group, housed at the University of Kansas. Katie is an experienced keynote speaker and gave her first TEDx in 2023. Her book with Page Two Publishing is expected in 2025.

Gabrielle Kotkov, MS, is an AMI 3–6 trained Montessori educator and consultant. She is the founder of Multilingual Montessori, where she shares resources about the intersection of multilingualism and Montessori education through presentations, consultations, and a podcast. She co-created the American Montessori Society's first self-paced course for educators, "Demystifying Multilingualism in Early Childhood." She is on the teaching faculty at the West Side Montessori School Teacher Education Program in NYC and the content development team at Trillium Montessori.

Gina Lofquist, MEd, is the senior director of education and strategic initiatives at AMS. She oversees the professional development and teacher education areas while also developing and implementing multiple strategic initiatives.

Jesmine Seechek Lok, a PhD candidate, is a former director of Beijing Heart & Mind Montessori Teacher Education Center in Beijing, China, which offers an AMS credential. She is currently the founder and director of Beijing AiSee Child Development Center and serves as AMS's Mandarin language operations consultant.

Sinead Meehan, PhD, is an assistant professor of elementary education at Ball State University in Muncie, Indiana. She is also a Montessori teacher educator, school consultant, and workshop presenter. Her interests include STEM education, teacher preparation, and professional development.

Amira Mogaji, EdD, is the assistant superintendent of curriculum, instruction, and assessment for Battle Creek Public Schools, Battle Creek, MI, and the AMS Board president.

Denise Monnier is the director of advocacy for the Montessori Public Policy Initiative (MPPI), where she devotes her time to supporting MPPI advocacy leads across the country as they advocate for policy change to increase access to Montessori. She is also the executive director of the Association of Illinois Montessori Schools. Denise was a Montessori child and has nearly 20 years of experience working in Montessori schools.

Jana Morgan Herman, MEd, is the director of the Montessori Institute of Teacher Education at Endeavor and the national director of Montessori education at Endeavor Schools, a community of 50 Montessori schools. She is a co-founder of the Kentucky Montessori Alliance and a Montessori historian and writer specializing in Montessori texts and current research on child development.

Elizabeth Park, PhD, is an associate professor and director of Early Childhood and Montessori Programs at Chaminade University of Honolulu (CUH). She earned her BS in Applied Mathematics from UCLA, an MA in Interior Design from Pratt Institute, an MEd in Early Childhood Education with a Montessori Credential from CUH, and a PhD in Educational Technology from the University of Hawai'i at Manoa. She is an AMS TEAC Commissioner and a co-chair of the AMS Research Committee.

Anna Perry, MEd, is the executive director of Seton Montessori Institute and Schools and serves as a presenter for all of Seton's academic programs. She is an expert on Montessori education, school leadership and administration, child development, and the Montessori philosophy. In addition to lecturing for Seton, she oversees the operations of Seton Montessori Institute, Seton Montessori School, and the Montessori Children's House of North Barrington.

Vanessa Rigaud, EdD, is an associate professor and program director at the Montessori Institute in the School of Education at Xavier University in Cincinnati, OH. Dr. Rigaud received her EdD in executive leadership at St. John Fisher College in Rochester, NY. Her research engages with curriculum development, culturally responsive teaching, and the intersections between Montessori-based research and teacher education. Dr. Rigaud has presented at various conferences and published articles/books nationwide and internationally.

Teresa Ripple, EdD, based in Saint Paul, MN, is an associate professor at St. Catherine University, and a former Montessori teacher and school executive director.

Laura Saylor, PhD, is the dean of the School of Education at Mount St. Joseph University in Cincinnati, OH. She holds a PhD in Educational Studies from the University of Cincinnati and an MEd from Xavier University. Laura has a diverse background in teaching and leadership, including serving as a teacher and school head. She is a regular presenter at national conferences, focusing her research on the intersection of cognitive science and Montessori education. Laura is also the co-author of *Powerful Literacy in the Montessori Classroom* and serves on the AMS board of directors.

Wendy Shenk-Evans, MDiv, is the former executive director of the Montessori Public Policy Initiative (MPPI) and a former head of school. She is an equity-driven collaborative leader, strategist, and early childhood education advocate.

Munir Shivji, MEd, is the American Montessori Society's executive director. For over 20 years, he has been a noteworthy leader in Montessori education— as a former teacher, instructor, school administrator, and teacher education program administrator.

Elizabeth Slade, MFA, is an author and educator with 36 years of experience working in Montessori education. She has worked in independent and public Montessori schools and spent 6 years at the National Center for Montessori in the Public Sector, working with public Montessori schools nationwide. She now serves as the executive director of Public Montessori in Action International, an organization created to ensure fully implemented Montessori education for children, families, and educators of the global majority. Her book *Montessori in Action: Building Resilient Montessori Schools* was released in July 2021, and her historical fiction novel *Momentum: Montessori, a Life in Motion* was released in August 2023. Elizabeth holds an AMI Elementary diploma, an AMS Montessori Administrators credential, and an MFA from Spalding University.

Martha Teien, MEd, is the founding director, owner, and Early Childhood lead guide of Mountain Montessori in Avon, CO, now in its 20th year. She is pursuing her Montessori doctoral degree from the University of Wisconsin River Falls. Martha is a parent-educator facilitator for the AMS international online class "You and Your Child's Montessori Education." She is also the president of the Montessori Public Policy Initiative (MPPI).

Zhuojing Zhang, MBA, is an Elementary teacher at BASIS Independent School in Fremont, CA. She is a doctoral student in the School of Education at Liberty University. She also works as a training teacher and a consultant in Fountainhead Montessori Adult Education (Dublin, CA), which offers an AMS credential.

ACKNOWLEDGMENTS

We thank all the authors of this book for the clarity, insights, and thoughtful scholarship they brought to the project. In addition, special recognition is given to Carey Jones, Dean Blase, Gina Lofquist, Heather Gerker, Marie Conti, Melanie Thiesse, Melina Papadimitriou, Munir Shivji, and the original authors of *Montessori in Contemporary American Culture*: Marlene Barron, Elizabeth Bronsil, Eileen Buermann, John Chattin-McNichols, Carol Chomsky, Betsy Coe, William Crain, David Elkind, David Kahn, Lilian Katz, Antonia Lopez, Ann Neubert, Nancy Rambusch, Sylvia Richardson, and Joy Turner (and the book's editor, Peggy Loeffler). Their invaluable contributions continue to inspire and guide our community.